She Writes for Him

Black
Voices of
Wisdom

She Writes for Him

Black Voices of Wisdom

ROMANS 8:28
BOOKS
AN IMPRINT OF REDEMPTION
PRESS

FEATURING AUTHORS AND SPEAKERS
MERCY LOKULUTU
ROBYN L. GOBIN, PH.D.
SHARON NORRIS ELLIOTT

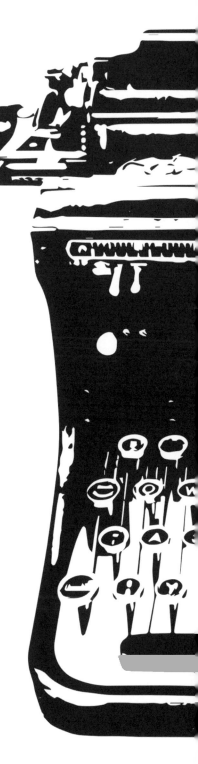

Published by She Writes for Him Books, a division of Redemption Press,
PO Box 427, Enumclaw, WA 98022
Toll-Free (844) 2REDEEM (273-3336)

She Writes for Him Books and Redemption Press are honored to present this title in partnership with the authors. She Writes for Him Books and Redemption Press provide our imprint seal representing design excellence, creative content, and high-quality production.

Scriptures marked AMP are taken from the AMPLIFIED BIBLE (AMP): Scripture taken from the AMPLIFIED® BIBLE, Copyright © 1954, 1958, 1962, 1964, 1965, 1987 by the Lockman Foundation Used by Permission. (www.Lockman.org)

Scriptures marked ESV are taken from THE HOLY BIBLE, ENGLISH STANDARD VERSION (ESV): Scriptures marked as NASB are taken from THE HOLY BIBLE, ENGLISH STANDARD VERSION ® Copyright© 2001 by Crossway, a publishing ministry of Good News Publishers. Used by permission.

Scriptures marked as "(GNT)" are taken from the Good News Translation—Second Edition © 1992 by American Bible Society. Used by permission.

Scriptures marked KJV are taken from the KING JAMES VERSION (KJV): KING JAMES VERSION, public domain.

Scriptures marked NIV are taken from the NEW INTERNATIONAL VERSION (NIV): Scripture taken from THE HOLY BIBLE, NEW INTERNATIONAL VERSION ®. Copyright© 1973, 1978, 1984, 2011 by Biblica, Inc.TM. Used by permission of Zondervan

Scriptures marked NKJV are taken from the NEW KING JAMES VERSION (NKJV): Scripture taken from the NEW KING JAMES VERSION®. Copyright© 1982 by Thomas Nelson, Inc. Used by permission. All rights reserved.

Scriptures marked NLT are taken from the HOLY BIBLE, NEW LIVING TRANSLATION (NLT): Scriptures taken from the HOLY BIBLE, NEW LIVING TRANSLATION, Copyright© 1996, 2004, 2007 by Tyndale House Foundation. Used by permission of Tyndale House Publishers, Inc., Carol Stream, Illinois 60188. All rights reserved. Used by permission.

Scripture quotations marked TPT are from The Passion Translation®. Copyright © 2017, 2018 by Passion & Fire Ministries, Inc. Used by permission. All rights reserved. ThePassionTranslation.com.

Printed in Korea

Dedication

To our Black sisters in Christ—in hopes that we may grow in our understanding of the ugliness of racism in our culture and seek to work together to create change.

Cynthia Cavanaugh
Managing Editor

TABLE OF CONTENTS

She Writes for Him
Black Voices of Wisdom

Introduction xi

One — Leadership in Racial Reconciliation 13
Mercy Lokulutu

Two — I Am a Woman of Color 19
Christina Custodio

Three — The Four Cs of Love and Leadership 25
Karynthia Phillips

Four — Raising Black Daughters 31
Dr. Evelyn Johnson-Taylor

Five — The Call 37
Cassandra Woods

Six — In the Middle of the Storm 43
Marva Titley-Smith

Seven — See Something, Say Something 49
Carol Chisolm

Eight	Overcoming *Dr. Grace Allman Burke*	55
Nine	Moving into Freedom *Tonya Williamson*	61
Ten	No Longer a Slave *Christina Custodio*	67
Eleven	Exclusion Tried, Inclusion Triumphs *Sharon Norris Elliott*	71
Twelve	Love Thy Neighbor *Kennita Williams*	77
Thirteen	No Room in the City *Laura Simon*	81
Fourteen	Strong in Christ *Robyn L. Gobin, PhD*	87
Fifteen	Finding Hope Again *Chelsi Bennett*	93
Sixteen	My Resting Place *Donna Pryor*	99
Seventeen	He Heals the Brokenhearted *Kenya Edwards*	103

Eighteen   Adopted by Two Fathers 109
                Rosemary Norris-Skates

Nineteen   Overcoming in Challenging Times 115
                Brenna J. Fields

Twenty   Leap of Faith 121
                LaShondria M. Smith

Twenty-One   Because His Blood Was Red 127
                Jamila Jenkins

Twenty-Two   Let It Shine 133
                Stacee P. Carr

Twenty-Three   The White Supremacist in Me 139
                Christina Custodio

                Resources 145
                Endnotes 147

Introduction

It was the first week of June, so the death of George Floyd was front and center in the news and at the top of the minds of many.

We were wrapping up one of the training calls for the She Writes for Him Bootcamp. Thirty-plus women, excited to learn how to tell their stories, were crammed onto a Zoom call.

Cynthia, from our She Writes team, directed her question to the lone Black sister in the group. "So, Laura, with everything going on, how are *you* doing?"

Long pause.

"Well, it's been hard. I struggle to find words to express my emotions. I'm crying a lot."

That began a raw conversation with our sister in Christ that opened our eyes to so many things.

How often those of us who are white say things to our Black sisters that unknowingly minimize their pain, don't value or celebrate our differences, or don't seek to learn from those who are different from us.

Then there are times when we, the white church in America, should stand up and speak out against the racial injustice we see around us, but we are eerily silent.

As Cynthia, Andi, and I as a team began unpacking what happened that night in the Bootcamp, we asked the question, "What can we do? How can we be part of the solution rather than just seeing a need and going back to business as usual?"

The first thing I felt compelled to do as the publisher was to film and promote a formal response from Redemption Press to the racial injustice that still exists, even in the church. After that I began inviting my Black sisters as guests to be interviewed on our All Things Podcast to share their personal experiences with racism, to help educate those of us who are white and often in the dark about what our Black sisters face on a regular basis.

We also wanted to give voice to those who at times get turned down by Christian publishers because of the color of their skin.

And so, this special edition of the *She Writes for Him* compilation was born. It is our hope that this volume introduces you to some new voices, touches your heart with compassion, and helps build a bridge between the white and Black churches in America today.

Welcome to *She Writes for Him: Black Voices of Wisdom*. We pray you are encouraged, inspired, and even challenged by the messages from these authors.

Athena Dean Holtz,
Publisher

Chapter One

Leadership in Racial Reconciliation

Mercy Lokulutu

I am a daughter of Nigerian soil. It has been said that Nigerians are bred with a "casual arrogance." I chuckle even typing that, knowing it is absolutely true. That adage speaks to the confidence of knowing the full breadth of your ancestral tapestry, and having your identity framed and sealed by a rich cultural tradition.

I attended an international school that was, for lack of a better term, a utopia of diversity. Students from all over the globe attended the school nestled in the vast basaltic plateaus of Jos. Within that unique community there was a celebration of *different* and *other*, not a fear of it. We had a yearly food festival that looked like a United Nations' cornucopia of delicacies: Ethiopian injera, Danish ØllebrØd, Nigerian suya, Lebanese shawarma, and Indian samosas all happily coexisting on our plates. I saw people being authentic, bringing their full selves to the table of friendship. Here was the caveat, there was room for everyone at the table.

Imagine my culture shock, then, upon moving to America as an eighteen-year-old and hearing the word *minority* for the first time in my sociology class in reference to gentrification against people who looked like me. Imagine my horror when reading about the Jim Crow era in a history textbook and trying to comprehend the diabolical systemic racism that exists in America. Imagine my heartbreak when

I am no stranger to injustice and the heinous rot of the fruit of racism.

I see how divided the church is over racism and how uncomfortable so many of my brothers and sisters in Christ are when acknowledging that my life matters, just . . . matters.

I am no stranger to injustice and the heinous rot of the fruit of racism. I have seen firsthand the brutal depravity of humanity in slave posts like Goree Island, Senegal. I have placed my hands on the prison bars of the cell that held Nelson Mandela captive as a political prisoner in the days of apartheid on Robben Island in South Africa. Our collective consciousness was shocked and pierced as we watched the grotesque images of a dying man utter words no mother wants to hear from her child, "I can't breathe."

However, what I have endured in America in the last few years, and in recent months, hits right where it hurts the most. I am reckoning with the heart-wrenching truth that my own son could be the next hashtag. This past summer, even while we were reeling from the effects of a global pandemic, my husband and I had "the talk" with my son. If you are thinking I am referring to the talk about "the birds and the bees," I wish you were right. We talked to my son about how he will present his blackness to a world that may see him as a threat just for existing.

My sorrow as a Black leader in the church comes from the silence of my friends when it comes to race relations in the church. Responses from some I consider brethren in Christ have varied from apathy to rejection of the very premise of racism at worst. Insult upon injury.

I am not saying my white brothers and sisters are a monolith; the response to the tension of racial injustice is divided. It seems some are only comfortable standing side by side in worship, but not willing to sit side by side in pain. I know God's original intent for the church is found in 1 Corinthians 12:14–27: one body united in its unique parts; when one part suffers, the others are to suffer with it. However, when the race and power inequities spark protests and rallies, I see an unwillingness from some of my white brothers and sisters to listen to the wounded. Instead, they choose to disparage, minimize, and dehumanize, rather than empathize. I am shocked to see Christian leaders reluctant to tease politics apart from social justice long enough to address race issues affecting those in their congregation who are not in the majority.

Sometimes, when pain is driving, anger is the copilot. Many times in the past months I have wrestled with reactions and opinions that force me to back off the ledge and onto my knees. I typed up incensed responses to posts, but even before my fingers could tap the send button, I knew I needed to humbly erase all of it at the gentle prodding of the Holy Spirit. For extended periods of time, I had to just stay off social media and zip my lips—easier said than done!

Thankfully, revelation is never more than a prayer away. I see that deeply entrenched in the racial division in our country it is not Black versus white but the kingdom of God versus the kingdom of darkness. The deeper issue here is not a left or right talking point. We need to stop taking sides and all meet in the middle and look up to Jesus.

We are tossed about with bias and spin, dizzy with rhetoric. It's a false dichotomy to feel we have to choose a side, Black lives or all lives. *False!* We can be for what God is for, weeping with those who weep *and* rejoicing with those who rejoice. We can occupy the space of loving the ninety-nine *and* also loving the one. We can be willing to sit with the woman at the well *and* the teachers of the law. It's not *either or*, it's *both and*. The only side that matters to me is reflecting heaven's heart. What does God think? There are too many voices claiming to be truth, only His matters.

As a Christian, my response to all the tension, the polarization, and toxic environments currently unfolding in America is to consistently ask the Lord, "How can I best represent you?" That prayer has never been more fervent or necessary. I don't write this from a moral high ground but rather an embodied repentance. If, like me, you are lamenting what has been revealed lately both in our world and in our hearts, can I just encourage you to allow the Lord to draw you completely into Himself and firmly

> I see that deeply entrenched in the racial division in our country it is not Black versus white but the kingdom of God versus the kingdom of darkness.

but lovingly reveal His heart? Your lament will become a prophetic cry that heaven hears because the Comforter is here.

Change starts with us. Take a step. Maybe for you that looks like leading with love and empathy, regardless of how you feel. Even if you don't know all the facts, even if your version of justice has not been served, even if you feel there is an agenda behind what is happening, allow love to bridge the gap.

For others that step may look like displaying mercy and forgiveness in the fight for justice. Sometimes in our quest to fight injustice, our stance tends to be judgmental, rather than merciful. Justice and mercy are not mutually exclusive. Jesus masterfully navigated the tension of both. God gave us Micah 6:8 (NIV) as a manifesto: "For He has shown you, O mortal, what is good. And what does the Lord require of you? To act justly and to love mercy and to walk humbly with your God." My rendering of this Scripture is that it's good to seek justice, but while you do so, be merciful, and tie it all together with humility. What a stunning picture of the stance we can take in the days we are in.

Take a step to listen to the wounded; equip yourself with books or podcasts from trusted voices with a sound biblical worldview who can challenge your thinking. Change starts with you, and includes repentance, listening, being willing, like the Good Samaritan, to move out of your comfort zone and have empathy for someone who doesn't look like you. Take the risk of bandaging their wounds, even if you don't fully understand the source of their pain, knowing full well you may get their blood, sweat, and tears on you, but helping anyway. This is the way forward.

As a Christian, my response to all the tension, the polarization, and toxic environments currently unfolding in America is to consistently ask the Lord, "How can I best represent you?"

➤ Wisdom Truth

He has shown you, O mortal, what is good. And what does the LORD require of you? To act justly and to love mercy and to walk humbly with your God. (Micah 6:8 NIV)

➤ Wisdom Prayer

Father, help us to reflect You with every interaction, every conversation, in thought and in deed. May we value life from the cradle to the grave and see everyone as the image bearer You created them to be. May justice and rightness flow on this side of eternity, in Jesus's name.

- How can you look at the issue of racism not as the kingdom of God versus the kingdom of darkness?
- How can you elevate this principle beyond the world's system?
- Practically, what does meeting in the middle and looking to Jesus mean to you?
- How will you take a step toward understanding the lived experience of someone who does not look like you?

_____

_____

_____

_____

_____

_____

_____

_____

_____

_____

Mercy Lokulutu is a preacher, teacher, and author who carries with her a rich cultural and spiritual heritage. She was ordained at Celebration Church in Florida in 2002 and is committed to building the local church globally, along with her husband, Marcus, and their three wonderful children, Isaiah, Ava-Pauline, and Zuri. In addition to speaking at conferences and churches around the world, Mercy is currently getting a master's degree in psychiatry as a nurse practitioner in Dallas. You can find her at mercylokulutu.com, Facebook/Mercy Lokulutu, and Instagram/mercylokulutu.

Chapter Two

I Am a Woman of Color

Christina Custodio

I know sometimes you might forget but . . . I am a woman of color in America.

I acknowledge I am privileged in many ways. I grew up in a middle-class family. I went to private school through high school, my parents are still married to each other, along with many other advantages. However, I wear brown skin each day whether I feel like it or not. Though I've never carried the literal weight of chains, I do bear psychological scars of enslavement. I know you see me with a smile on my face that radiates confidence, but the truth that lies behind the smile might surprise you.

When I was a little girl (well, it started when I was a little girl) I thought I was ugly. I felt no one could see the beauty in me unless they had brown skin and looked the way I did.

When I was fifteen my best friend said, "I think God made a mistake when He made you Black. You should have been white."

Whoa.

The sad thing is, I agreed with her. He must have made a mistake. How did I end up in this skin? Today my heart breaks for that young girl who couldn't see the beauty in herself. I wish I could go back to her, wrap my arms around her brown shoulders and tell her how gifted she is, how beautiful she is, and how God doesn't make mistakes.

My parents loved me and did the best they could to help me see my potential. But my Southern California world of magazines and TV and Christian private school told me people who looked like me were either criminals and thugs, or they were rich comedians, singers, or athletes whose only purpose was to entertain.

So who was I? Who did they think I was? Who did God say I was?

Though I always had a smile on my face (in fact, I won "best smile" in eighth grade and "best laugh" in twelfth grade), I carried the pain of feeling worthless.

Isn't it sad we seek validation from those who don't even truly know us while disregarding those who do, who love us unconditionally?

Each year in history class I dreaded studying the "slave chapter." As one of the only Black girls, I knew everyone would turn and look at me wondering what it was like to be a slave.

I wanted to scream at them, "I don't know, you idiots! I grew up just like you! Stop looking at me!"

Latasha Morrison, author of *Be the Bridge*, hit the nail on the head when she said people look to the person of color to speak up for themselves when racial injustice happens, which in itself can feel oppressive. Imagine if those who are not of color spoke up and out for their brothers and sisters who are.

I know that would have made all the difference for me growing up—and would even now.

Though I have come so far in developing a healthy relationship with the color of my skin, I still sometimes struggle with the fear of not knowing if someone will look at me with disdain because my melanin levels make them uncomfortable.

Isn't it sad we seek validation from those who don't even truly know us, while disregarding those who do, who love us unconditionally?

Jennie Allen, in her book *Get Out of Your Head*, talks about when we choose to believe lies about ourselves, it is at least one of these three lies: "I am helpless, I am worthless, I am unlovable."

When I read that, I thought to myself, *Nope! Not me, I don't have a problem with any of that!* Then I thought about how I sometimes still have difficulty believing people like me, much less love me. There are times when I feel they just need me for something or want something out of me. I do understand that's a lie from Satan, but I didn't realize until very recently that I fight a daily battle against the lie that I am unlovable.

Please don't tell me, "I don't see color." It's not true, and it doesn't make me feel loved and accepted. *See me.*

Friends, it goes deep. It goes back to the white boy who liked me but would never tell me or anybody else because I wasn't the right color. It goes back to being called the n-word just because someone felt he had a right. It goes back to being followed through a store because the media led them to believe the involuntary "uniform" I wear is one of a thief.

However, I know who the real thief is. "The thief comes only to steal and kill and destroy" (John 10:10 NIV). His name is Satan, and he is a liar.

I am a woman of color.

Please don't tell me, "I don't see color." It's not true, and it doesn't make me feel loved and accepted. *See me.* I have brown skin. It may be different from yours, and that is okay. In fact, it's more than okay. It's phenomenal. Acknowledge and embrace our diversity. God created it, and it is beautiful! Let's celebrate it!

I will sing the song of David who exclaims, "I praise you for I am fearfully and wonderfully made. Wonderful are your works; my soul knows it very well" (Psalm 139:14 ESV). Today I recognize I am beautiful because I am created by a God of beauty who doesn't make mistakes. Today I embrace the gifts I have. Today I accept my place as a child of God. I am royalty. I am valuable. I am chosen. Don't you know you are too?

But you are a chosen race, a royal priesthood, a holy nation, a people for his own possession, that you may proclaim the excellencies of him who called you out of darkness into his marvelous light. (1 Peter 2:9 ESV)

Wisdom Prayer

Dear Heavenly Father, You tell me in Your Word that I am fearfully and wonderfully made. Sometimes it is so very hard to believe that. The Enemy whispers such believable lies in my ear. Lord, help me hear Your voice loud and clear. Your joy is my strength. I will walk tall and strong in the knowledge that I am Yours. You have set me apart to use my gifts to do great things for Your kingdom. Thank You for Your Holy Spirit who continues to guide me, showing me the path You have laid before me. Thank You, Lord, for all You are and all I am in You.

I am royalty. I am valuable. I am chosen. Don't you know you are too?

⁓ Wisdom Reflection

- What have you believed about yourself that isn't true?
- What steps will you take to stop believing those lies and embrace God's truth about who you really are?

_____
_____
_____
_____
_____
_____
_____
_____
_____
_____
_____
_____
_____
_____
_____
_____

Christina Custodio is a wife and mother of three. She is the founder of Agapeland Ministries, dedicated to inspiring women to find joy regardless of their circumstances. She is currently working on a book recounting the forty-four days she lived in a hospital following her son's near death. Visit Christina at christinacustodio.com.

Chapter Three

The Four Cs of Love and Leadership
Karynthia Phillips

Success for a Black woman in a world whose value of humanity is predicated on gender and race requires personal values of courage, conviction, creativity, and collaboration with man and God.

Walk down "Memory Lane" with me to my awakening and first awareness of racism. As a child, I was raised in a home in a diverse community that demonstrated unity among Blacks, whites, and Puerto Ricans. Acts of solidarity became second nature for me as far back as my childhood memories of a house full of females, with my mother demonstrating faith, hope, and unconditional love as a community matriarch. The Lord had shown her what was required of her: to act justly, love mercy, and to walk humbly with her God (Micah 6:8 NIV).

Our small home included my five sisters, two brothers, one or two aunts, two female cousins, and runaways or the evicted that showed up from time to time. My parents divorced when I was only thirteen and in the ninth grade (yes, I was that young). I often wondered what my father was thinking as he dealt with rooms full of females. Too often he would simply make a 180-degree turn, shaking his head.

In those formative years I began to see the power the Armstrong women possessed. I quickly learned the importance of role models who provided a blueprint

Although we recognized
differences in the
community, we were
taught to value all of
humanity.

for tenacity, a life of knowing right and wrong, creative survival skills, sisterly support, and unity. Although we recognized differences in the community, we were taught to value all of humanity.

Kitchen creativity stirred in the pots and in us as we chatted about dreams and visions. My mother was a community parent on patrol who consoled battered women, fed hungry children, and spanked disorderly ones, often saying, "Now go home and tell your mother I did it."

Growing up in New Haven, Connecticut, I was not aware of the oppression of blatant racism in the 1960s. When President John F. Kennedy was assassinated, I observed the sadness and tears of both Black and white people. Televised desegregation marches led by Dr. Martin Luther King Jr., his speeches, and his assassination did not resonate with me and the challenges of my diverse community. During the Black Power movement, the Black Panthers were active in my neighborhood, and I began to realize how people were treated differently based on skin color. As the Black Panthers became prominent, their presence was felt everywhere through a barrage of signs and billboards, free breakfasts, tutoring after school, and resources to address other social inequities. Children, including me, were escorted to school by these "giant" Black men with black berets and uniforms and other security paraphernalia, causing my young brown eyes to be filled with fear and wonderings.

I remember waking up in the middle of the night to another riot, sirens blaring, the breaking of glass, and blazing fire and smoke that pierced through the darkness. Across the street I could hear a man trapped in a burning storefront, screaming for his life. His voice had an unimaginable cry of fear. After our family was rescued by the National Guard, I remember waking up in the home of a white family. They were smiling and saying, "They are beautiful," while my parents peered into our faces to assure us of their presence. We were displaced for a few days before returning home.

Looking back at my elementary through college years, I cannot recall ever having experiences of flagrant racism. However, at my first chapel service at Fisk University in Nashville, Tennessee, tears streamed down my face as my ears and heart heard the lyrics of the Black national anthem, "Lift Every Voice and Sing" by James Weldon Johnson. In that moment I received greater understanding, or revelation, if you will, of the "weary years" and "silent tears."

We are all human, but I wondered why my people were treated so badly. The heritage of who I was and who I was becoming evolved, and I was proud of my tears. America's Christian disunity, nonetheless, escaped me. Despite this, I made the conscious choice to maintain my conviction and stay true to the second commandment of Jesus to "love thy neighbor as thyself" (Matthew 22:39 KJV).

There is an African proverb that says, "If you want to go fast, go alone; but if you want to go far, go together."

The gifting of leadership began to blossom in me as I read biographies of great women of all heritages. One stayed in the forefront of my memory: abolitionist Harriet Tubman (Araminta Ross) who obtained her freedom against all odds and went back to her community to liberate her family and others who wanted to escape from slavery. Recently, as my husband and I watched the movie *Harriet*, I took note of mutual leadership qualities (courage, conviction, creativity, and collaboration with man and God). We two women of leadership both possess solitude and discontentment with our success unless other lives we touch are empowered to pursue doors of hope and a life of liberty. Harriet Tubman is quoted as saying, "Every great dream begins with a dreamer. Always remember, you have within you the strength, the patience, and the passion to reach for the stars to change the world."

The *Harriet* movie provoked the memories of systemic racism experienced through encounters with two white Christian professors. At two different professional schools, and nearly ten years apart, I encountered the lack of faith in me of one teacher who assured me no one of my color could pass the board examination or obtain employment. The other, a mentor and instructor whose Christian love professed "white privilege," compared me to the entire class to the stereotypically negative verbiage of being an "angry Black woman" because of my convictions. A note left on my desk at one of the schools simply read "KKK." The constant doubting of my capabilities kept the horror of racism ever present throughout those years. Among the twenty students, three whites failed, I passed and obtained

There is an African proverb that says, "If you want to go fast, go alone; but if you want to go far, go together."

> The oppressive spirit of racism will eventually create frustration that leads to engaging in unfruitful arguments, succumbing to intimidation, and ultimately neglecting your gifts and talents if you forget your purpose and God-given assignment in life.

employment within a month of graduation. In my second experience, God kept proving to the mentor that I produced successful projects despite her lackluster support.

My motives and intelligence were being minimized by two respected leaders because of my gender and race. I am not even sure they realized what they were doing. The apostle Paul instructed Timothy about the do's and don'ts of godly leaders in 1 Timothy 4:6–16:

- Do not waste time arguing about foolishness and silly myths (4:7).
- Do not be intimidated by being a youth . . . a novice in any aspect (4:12).
- Do not neglect your gift (4:14).

The oppressive spirit of racism will eventually create frustration that leads to engaging in unfruitful arguments, succumbing to intimidation, and ultimately neglecting your gifts and talents if you forget your purpose and God-given assignment in life. The caveat I learned is to take courage, never let despair and the emotions of fear lead your decisions (see Joshua 1:9).

Paul emphasized the infrastructure of the Four Cs of leadership: courage, conviction, creativity, and collaboration.

- Courage: In everything you do, model godliness (1 Timothy 4:12).
- Conviction: Continue to study, preach, and teach the Bible (4:6, 13).
- Creativity: Keep spiritually sensitive to God (4:7–11).
- Collaboration: Stay aware of how you represent Christ (4:16).

The foundation of our racist society has shaped every girl and boy who have been nurtured in the "American Way." It is enmeshed in our institutions and thus in our response to the structures that have honed this great country. Sisters, never socially distance yourself because of the differences you see in another person. All have sinned and have fallen short of the glory of God, whether by an act of omission or commission. It will take humble hearts full of courage, conviction, collaboration, and creativity to produce a worthy response, while leading by example in God's call to love one another. Anaïs Nin wrote, "And the time came when the risk to remain tight in a bud was more painful than the risk it took to blossom."

~ Wisdom Truth

> Have I not commanded you? Be strong and courageous. Do not be frightened, and do not be dismayed, for the Lord your God is with you wherever you go. (Joshua 1:9 ESV)

~ Wisdom Prayer

> *Lord*, teach me to lead by example by demonstrating love to all of humanity.

Sisters, never socially distance yourself because of the differences you see in another person.

- Take some time to learn about a race or culture of Americans that are of different descent. Then consider a direct response in your community (at a cultural event or volunteer or support a worthy cause).
- Talk with family members of different generations and assess their core values on systemic racism. Then make an effort to learn about "white privilege."
- Reflect on what you have learned and determine how you will lead differently in a community and country that is diverse.

Karynthia Glasper-Phillips is a speaker and author whose workshops integrate the importance of beginning with self-care of spirit, mind, and body for effectiveness in life. She is a healthcare practitioner and adjunct professor at American Baptist College. Highlights of her days are when women walk beyond their boundaries into the life God designed for them.

Chapter Four

Raising Black Daughters
Dr. Evelyn Johnson-Taylor

The pink sweater, plaid dress, and white bobby socks on our six-year-old daughter said it all. The finishing touches of styling her hair like Ruby Bridges would be the hardest part to completing our preparations. Jade was born with a headful of jet-black hair, and it was getting thicker by the day. By the time she was two, braiding her hair was an overwhelming, all-day project. But not today. This would be a good hair day.

Emboldened and determined, our daughter was perfect for this role. With her larger-than-life personality, Jade would tell a new audience about Ruby Bridges, a bright six-year-old chosen to be the first African American student to integrate her local New Orleans elementary school.

With a bowl of hot cereal and fresh fruit for breakfast, book bags gathered, lunches made, and what to say prepared, the day was off to a grand start. In her outfit, Jade looked like Ruby. *The Story of Ruby Bridges* was a frequent read in our home. Jade understood the message we emphasized from the story. Today she was not only a Black first grader in a predominantly white, private Christian school, but she was also about to present the story of a civil rights activist. The smile on her

Being able to identify with accomplished people who looked like her reinforced what we taught her: that she could do anything she set her mind to.

face told me she was ready. Snapping the pink bow in her hair, I headed with her out the door.

Our daughters' school had asked each student to dress like a historical figure. Ours was an intentional choice to further affirm our daughter's identity. Being able to identify with accomplished people who looked like her reinforced what we taught her: that she could do anything she set her mind to. As a bonus, Jade would share some lesser-known Black history with her classmates. Most of the children in her class had heard stories about Dr. Martin Luther King Jr., the Montgomery bus boycott, and Harriet Tubman aiding enslaved people on their journey through the Underground Railroad. Jade sharing with her classmates how one brave little girl, Ruby Bridges, changed the course of history would be eye-opening to the other first graders.

The anxiety Ruby's parents must have felt, wondering if they were doing the right thing by agreeing to use their daughter to desegregate an all-white school. On November 14, 1960, federal marshals drove Ruby and her mother, Lucille, to her new school, five blocks from her home. The innocence of her youth probably rendered her unaware of the hate and racism toward her as they walked through the angry mob into the school, but not her parents. I'm not sure I could have willingly exposed my first grader to such vile hatred, but Ruby's bravery showed the world the influence children have to bring about change. She also showed me, as a mother of Black daughters, the significance of a child's voice. Having our daughter depict the role of a history maker ignited a new confidence in her.

We knew our daughters would face obstacles based on our choices of where we lived and what schools we sent them to. Having them grow up surrounded by children who look different meant we had to be deliberate and focused in our parenting. How do you tell a child they can do anything, while also telling them some doors won't be open to them because of their skin tone? They didn't need to know that they would encounter teachers who wouldn't expect much from them because they are Black. Or did they?

As parents, it was our responsibility to make our children aware that some people would have preconceptions of them. Their job was to prove wrong everyone who unfairly made assumptions about their capabilities based on color. When a teacher dismissed our daughter's request for help on an assignment, was it an over-worked teacher? Or was it because the teacher didn't expect much from the Black girl whose parents told her she could do anything?

To show our daughters that we would acknowledge their voices, we addressed every issue brought to our attention. We dismissed nothing. We needed to err on the side of caution, so we spent many hours in consultation with teachers, principals, and other parents. We encouraged adults in our circle to educate themselves to better understand the plight of Black Americans. We admonished those adults to look within and to speak up when they witnessed injustice.

When our daughters' school decided to remain open for Martin Luther King Jr. Day, despite it being a federal holiday, we spoke to the administrator. We voiced how important it was that our daughters and other Black students see this day receiving the same respect as other federal holidays. We decided not to send our children to school that day, and the school agreed not to count them absent. Later, the school closed for Martin Luther King Jr. Day.

When Jade was told she couldn't play the lead role in a production because the primary character was white, we made time to watch Brandy, a Black actress, star in the lead role of Rodgers & Hammerstein's *Cinderella*. We wanted Jade to see a Black actress take a role white stars had traditionally played. When our younger daughter's teacher questioned if her exceptional writing skills were authentic, it was imperative that we emphasized to Ebony never to dim her light just so someone else's could shine. We encouraged them both to be the most confident person in a room. Not the loudest, but the most self-assured. We taught them the importance of using their voices to speak out when they witnessed any injustice.

God created humans in all sizes, shapes, and colors. Nothing is missing from His creation. Instilling a sense of identity in our children at an early age was vital if we wanted them to become

Ruby's bravery showed the world the influence children have to bring about change.

confident adults. It was our job as parents to affirm that their differences made them beautiful, that God's creativity in creation was something to be embraced and admired. It was vital that we affirm from the beginning that their uniqueness expresses God's great love and that He didn't make a mistake. Their skin tone was intentional. We taught them, "Even if you are the only Black person in a room, don't make yourself small or give your voice to anyone else." We wanted our daughters to see the different colors of people and be confident in who God created them to be.

When a person says, "I don't see color," it prevents that person from recognizing racial difference and, by extension, racial oppression. Scholars have referred to this as "colorblind racism." When we see the unique colors of people, we can see the disparity in treatment of people and the beauty of each individual.

We stressed to our daughters to never be ashamed of who they are. When others seek to make them feel small, they need to know their worth.

Both our daughters are unapologetic, intelligent, and secure Black women making a difference in their culture. One holds a master's of science-student affairs in higher education with a concentration in diversity, equity, and dialogue. The other has two history degrees with a concentration in African American history.

While much of the conversation today, and rightfully so, is on Black sons and the racism they face in America, it is important that we don't forget that Black daughters give birth to legacy. A poised woman who celebrates who God created her to be will influence generations to come. Empower her while she is young by giving voice to her concerns.

God created humans in all sizes, shapes, and colors. Nothing is missing from His creation.

⌁ Wisdom Truth

For you created my inmost being; you knit me together in my mother's womb. I praise you because I am fearfully and wonderfully made; your works are wonderful, I know that full well. My frame was not hidden from you when I was made in the secret place, when I was woven together in the depths of the earth. Your eyes saw my unformed body. (Psalm 139:13–16 NIV)

⌁ Wisdom Prayer

Father, thank You for the privilege to mother Your creation. I pray for wisdom to impart truth to future generations in a way that speaks to their value. Help me show them by example that all are precious in Your sight. Thank You for taking careful thought in every part of creating us in Your image. Thank You that the hands of a loving God made each of us. Father, I pray that no person ever feels less important because of the color of their skin, but that all experience Your great love. In Jesus's name, I pray. Amen.

A poised woman who celebrates who God created her to be will influence generations to come.

- How important is identity in the war against racism? A firm sense of value doesn't mean that one won't experience outward discrimination. It was important to us that our children develop a solid foundation, affirming who God created them to be, hopefully giving them the skills to navigate the challenges of being Black in America, and the voice to speak for those who cannot speak for themselves. White America may never fully accept our daughters as equals, but it's important that they know God created them, and in His eyes, all are equal. One race: human. Those who are sincere in their quest for racial equality will seek to learn from history. Education is one of our best tools. It teaches us to be empathetic regarding others' experiences.
- How can you educate yourself regarding racism?
- How can you help bring unity?

Dr. Evelyn Johnson-Taylor is an author, speaker, theology professor, ordained minister, and a certified coach. She has served as a women's ministry leader since 1994 and is passionate about encouraging, empowering, and equipping women to win in life. She believes each woman has a purpose-focused dream, and she wants to help her make it a reality. Visit her at evelynjtaylor.org, Twitter/drevetaylor, and Instagram/drevetaylor.

Chapter Five

The Call

Cassandra Woods

The phone rang. I answered.

My life changed. Forever.

One decision, one comment, one action, and in my case, one diagnosis. Yes, the voice on the other end of the phone was my doctor.

After noticing a lump in my breast, I made an appointment with a doctor and soon found myself getting prepped for a biopsy as an outpatient. Now I was home. Though I somewhat understood the process, it never registered in my mind that I might get an unfavorable report.

When the doctor spoke to me on the phone, he seemed cold and distant. Of course, that wasn't true. There was no difference in his demeanor, but the way he delivered the news as if it was just another day at the office was shocking. Where was the kind, gentle doctor who I had become comfortable with? Was it protocol to deliver such news over the phone?

He said, "Ms. Woods, your report came back positive. Your tumor is malignant."

I never thought I'd hear my name and that word in the same sentence.

After hanging up the phone, I sat down. I was in shock. *Cancer? Me? Is this some kind of dream or a cruel joke?* I thought about my husband, who was traveling back into town. I didn't want to call him with the news.

I thought of my children, who were playing in a different room.

Then there were my parents, and I wasn't ready to go down that road.

And then my thoughts turned to God, King of Kings and Lord of Lords. I had a solid relationship with the Lord. I was still learning and growing, but I loved Him, and I knew He loved me. So I talked to Him, and I listened.

Since that day we've done a lot of talking and listening. I asked Him to tell me what He wanted me to do. I understood that everyone has either had the experience or knows someone who has. All too often they are ready and willing to offer the advice of what their "Aunt Sue" did when it happened to her.

It's been twenty years since this journey began.

Like cancer, racism has a way of infiltrating the soul of humanity to wreak havoc, sometimes quietly without being recognized, and sometimes in blatant, in-your-face attacks.

Either way, the damage can be undeniable and extensive as it invades, seeping into tiny cracks and crevices, leaving indelible impressions on young minds and aged souls, and even physical bodies.

Slavery and sharecropping, institutions that built up an empire for some, left others severely lacking in the ability to play full out in an economy set up to systematically keep them down. During and after the Reconstruction, when people were able to prove they could do something on their own to compete, various atrocities were allowed to trip them up. The Tulsa Race Massacre in 1921 is a prime example. It occurred when many Blacks and successful Black businesses located in the Greenwood District of Tulsa, Oklahoma, were attacked. The area never fully recovered.

Then along comes a situation like George Floyd's murder. The officer, cool, calm, and collected, assisted in the life flowing right out of Mr. Floyd. This was

> Like cancer, racism has a way of infiltrating the soul of humanity to wreak havoc, sometimes quietly without being recognized, and sometimes in blatant, in-your-face attacks.

one of those times that demanded the attention of the world. Like the doctor's call I'd received one spring day, Floyd's death marked a point in history that will forever be etched in our minds. Like BC and AD, there will be a distinct difference in the way events of the world are categorized going forward, depending on whether or not the event occurred before or after Floyd's death.

Like a heart that skips a beat or flutters, the rhythm of life is interrupted when racism is allowed to play out its full course.

Atrial fibrillation is a condition that usually includes shortness of breath and an abnormal heart rhythm until the system is brought back into order, usually by some type of medication.

Oftentimes when cancer cells grow out of control, they travel to other areas of the body and begin to grow there. This is called metastatic disease. These cells are able to influence the cells around them to provide blood supply and nutrients to enable them to continue their devastation to the body they reside in. If the immune system is healthy, it will begin to fight against the cancer cells to return the body to health.

The fight is just as real against racist organizations that spew hateful propaganda and encourage others to spread their message. Using their influence, members of these organizations are able to get into the minds of vulnerable people and cause them to speak out and take actions that are detrimental to many.

This is what I believe happened with white supremacist Dylann Roof who murdered nine people in 2015 at a Bible study at Emanuel African Methodist Episcopal Church in Charleston, South Carolina.

A dose of truth can combat the lies that support the philosophy of racism and perhaps reduce the ability of such organizations to negatively affect more people.

Many of the initial protests after George Floyd's murder were really an effort to force anyone who could do something to help bring some order to a system that allowed such a terrible thing to happen.

Order is important to a system. God has so graciously given us an example of this in our own bodies. He has divinely orchestrated human beings with many parts that operate as one cohesive unit. When this doesn't happen as designed, our bodies are considered out of balance and fail to operate at an optimum level.

Each of our bodies make up a system that has many parts, and each of our bodies is also part of a bigger system. Within the body's system is a head, a nose, arms, legs, toes, and more. They each have a role to play. There is diversity at both a macro and a micro level within the divine systems God has created. Imagine the chaos that would erupt if the hand protested the foot being a part of the body because it didn't look like or act like the hand. Or what if the mouth declared the ears unimportant because they didn't process information the same way.

Each human body and its parts is divinely created and never considered dispensable by God. Whether "Jew or Gentile, slave or free" (1 Corinthians 12:13 NIV), or Black or white, this is true. "God has put the body together, giving greater honor to the parts that lacked it, so that there should be no division in the body, but that its parts should have equal concern for each other" (1 Corinthians 12:24–25 NIV). Like every fingerprint, our gifts and talents are unique and designed to make their own contribution to the world.

In an effort to spur on change in this area of race, we must not be so close-minded and unwilling to see ourselves not as bad people, but as people that possibly hold to some unhealthy beliefs. Let's forget about pointing fingers and start focusing on ourselves. Ask the hard questions and answer truthfully. "Search me, God, and know my heart; test me and know my anxious thoughts. See if there is any offensive way in me, and lead me in the way everlasting" (Psalm 139:23–24 NIV).

Let's not be so passionate about our positions and our politics that we fail to have eyes to see and ears to hear what God is doing. In the words of Robin S. Sharma, "Change is hard at first, messy in the middle, and gorgeous at the end."

A dose of truth can combat the lies that support the philosophy of racism.

So there is hope. It is all about answering the call when God dials your number. He may just say something that will change your life forever.

⌇ Wisdom Truth

So do not fear, for I am with you; do not be dismayed, for I am your God. I will strengthen you and help you; I will uphold you with my righteous right hand. (Isaiah 41:10 NIV)

⌇ Wisdom Prayer

Lord God, help us overcome our fears so we may evaluate our individual beliefs and bring them into agreement with Your truth. Grant us Your wisdom and courage to replace the thoughts that are not aligned with Your heart by thinking on things that are good and true, pure and righteous, excellent and praiseworthy.

Let's not be so passionate about our positions and our politics that we fail to have eyes to see and ears to hear what God is doing.

- Do you want to be well?
- Are you willing to examine yourself?
- Are you ready to take up your cross and take a stand?

Cassandra Woods is an inspirational author, speaker, and transformation coach. She is committed to supporting women desiring to move from simple existence to victorious living. The author of *Rise Up: Keys to Overcoming*, she has been married to her college sweetheart, Christopher, for thirty-six years, and they have four adult children and three grandchildren. Learn more at cassandrawoods.com, Instagram/cassandrawoodsbooks, and Facebook/cassandrawoodsbooks.

Chapter Six

In the Middle of the Storm
Marva Titley-Smith

Trust in the LORD forever, for the LORD, the LORD himself, is the Rock eternal.
ISAIAH 26:4 NIV

When the light poured into the room, I was sure our roof was gone. The water had already started pooling on the floor outside the closet door, and I wondered how much longer it would be before it reached our ankles. The banging had stopped, so perhaps this was our chance to make a run for it. I whispered to my husband, who was huddled with our daughter on the other side of the closet, "Do you think we can try now?"

"Yes, I think so."

But when I saw my car, I knew we wouldn't make it. It was as if some giant hand had snatched it up and dropped it carelessly across the driveway. Debris was strewn everywhere. Strips of roof sheeting and broken tree limbs mingled with the broken glass from the car windows. And that wind. The howling just wouldn't stop.

Our only choice was to go back into the closet. We had to wait this one out.

It's not that I'm unfamiliar with storms. In fact, where I live, we have a whole season—a full five months—earmarked for storms. Some of my earliest

I know storms well.
But this storm was
different.

memories involve the six of us kids inside a boarded-up house waiting out a storm with our parents. Safe and secure inside, we would occasionally crack the windows ever so slightly to get a peek at the storm, but it had to be timed just right for fear of blowing out the windows. In the eye of the storm, my mother would excitedly venture out during the lull to catch a glimpse of the damage. Once there was a massive yacht lying on its side in the middle of the road outside our window.

In my young-adult years I reveled in religiously tracking storms with my father. The coordinates of each named storm that made its way off the African coast and into the Caribbean Sea were painstakingly plotted on the yellowing map, its corners curled with wear. It became a ritual I looked forward to each year and a blessed memory of my dear father years after he was gone.

So I know storms well. But this storm was different.

Those might also have been Peter's words in Matthew 14:22–33, as he eyed the dark figure walking on the water toward the boat. There was something indeed different about that storm, for life, as Peter knew it, was about to change.

Scripture tells us the boat was far out to sea, buffeted by the waves. They were swayed and battered by the raging seas, and struggling at the oars. Amid all the commotion a "ghost" appeared, walking on the water.

Seeing their fear, Jesus told them to "take courage." Could this really be Jesus? Peter had to know for himself.

> "Lord, if it's you," Peter replied, "tell me to come to you on the water."
>
> "Come," he said.
>
> Then Peter got down out of the boat, walked on the water and came toward Jesus. But when he saw the wind, he was afraid and, beginning to sink, cried out, "Lord, save me!"
>
> Immediately Jesus reached out his hand and caught him. "You of little faith," he said, "why did you doubt?"

And when they climbed into the boat, the wind died down. Then those who were in the boat worshiped him, saying, "Truly you are the Son of God." (Matthew 14:28–33 NIV)

In the midst of a storm, Peter faced his fears and did what none besides Jesus had done. Peter miraculously walked on water. I'm sure Peter would have loved the story to finish right then and there. No one would notice if the storyteller quickly skipped to the next scene. But I believe what happened next was recorded, not to embarrass Peter, but to empower those of us who would read it and believe.

Peter's brief sojourn into the water-walking business teaches us three lessons that will help us thrive in any storm—if we follow them.

- When we are afraid, Jesus invites us into His presence (Matthew 14:27–29). Whether yours is a literal or figurative storm, you don't have to face it alone. God wants you to take courage and walk with Him. He is right there with you, as He was with Peter, ready to catch you if you fall.
- When we take our eyes off Jesus, we become overwhelmed by the storms of life (Matthew 14:30). Peter was boldly walking in faith until he shifted his focus back on the storm. As a result, the storm became bigger than Peter's faith. By keeping our eyes fixed on the One who stills the storm, we will trust God to keep us firm and secure.
- Every storm serves a purpose (Matthew 14:33). In Peter's case, the storm served to strengthen not just Peter's faith, but that of the disciples as well. There's a lesson in every storm. How we respond to the storms in our lives will impact those around us.

I can't pretend to know what storm you are facing right now, and I certainly don't want to make light of it. However, I believe God gave us Peter's example and those of other biblical characters to point us to the Rock Eternal.

Whether yours is a literal or figurative storm, you don't have to face it alone.

I can't say we came
out unscathed, but our
faith has certainly
grown stronger because
of the storm.

It's possible you're facing a storm similar to Peter's. Or maybe you can relate more to Job who faced storms of other-worldly proportions. Yet, when hit by the storm, Job praised God (Job 13:15).

Or how about Joseph? He was hit by one storm of betrayal after another but was able to acknowledge that God used it all for good (Genesis 50:20).

Then there's King Jehoshaphat who was so overwhelmed by the vast army coming against him that he cried out to God. His storm seemed bigger than his faith until he fixed his eyes on God (2 Chronicles 20:12). These heroes of the faith trusted God to see them through their storms.

My storm story might pale in comparison to those penned in the Bible, but I am beyond grateful for how God spared our lives. Hurricane Irma was the strongest hurricane ever to be recorded in the Atlantic Ocean. It touched down in our islands as a category 5 hurricane, the first for the region, and maintained a wind speed at or above a whopping 185 miles per hour for thirty-seven hours.

During those harrowing hours in the closet, we prayed and cried out to God. We kept our eyes on Him, and He did not let us down. I can't say we came out unscathed, but our faith has certainly grown stronger because of the storm. Yes, every storm has a purpose.

~ Wisdom Truth

Trust in the LORD forever, for the LORD, the LORD himself, is the Rock eternal. (Isaiah 26:4 NIV)

～ Wisdom Prayer

Father God, I am so grateful that You are still in the business of calming the seas and stilling the storms. In this world there is so much that threatens to overpower me, but You are my safe harbor. You are my sure hope. You are my Rock Eternal. I thank You for sending Your Son as an anchor for my soul. Help me to keep my eyes fixed on You and trust You to bring me safely through.

～ Wisdom Reflection

Friend, it might seem that your storm is too big for you to handle, but our God is bigger than any storm. With your eyes fixed on the Savior, you will never walk alone. If you're wondering what it looks like to fix your eyes on Jesus, consider these actions:

- Spend time in God's presence daily by reading His Word.
- Make prayer a priority and include it in your daily routine.
- Tell others of God's goodness.
- Ask God to show you the purpose in your storm.
- Thank God for your many blessings; yes, name them one by one.
- Praise God in the good times and the bad.

In this world there is so much that threatens to overpower me, but You are my safe harbor.

When storms arise how do you respond? Do you respond in faith with your eyes fixed on Jesus or in fear with your eyes focused on the storm? Are you going through a storm right now? What do you sense God teaching you through it? How can you trust in the Rock Eternal?

_____

_____

_____

_____

_____

_____

_____

_____

_____

_____

_____

_____

_____

_____

_____

_____

_____

Marva Titley-Smith is a management consultant and work-life coach who empowers women to thrive beyond the nine to five. She lives in the Virgin Islands with her husband of seventeen years and their two teenage children. Connect with Marva at MarvaSmith.com and on social media at @marvatsmith.

Chapter Seven

See Something, Say Something

Carol Chisolm

An old proverb says, "See no evil, hear no evil, speak no evil." Although the origin of the proverb is unknown, in Eastern cultures it is associated with the ability to dwell on good thoughts. On the contrary, in the Western world it refers to a lack of moral responsibility and the refusal to acknowledge acts of evil.

Countless incidents involving racism are unreported each year. In a report from the Department of Justice, more than half of crimes involving race are not reported to authorities. This is quite an alarming statistic.

If we witness the purse snatching of an elderly woman, we might chase after the offender to attempt to retrieve the stolen bag. If we walk by the local corner market and see a robbery in process with the storeowner held at gunpoint, we would not turn away and ignore the offense. We would rush safely around the corner and without hesitation dial 911 to alert the authorities.

Why are we apathetic when we witness blatant acts of racism? Why are we suddenly struck with blindness, deafness, and muteness and refuse to get involved?

All too often those victimized by racism fail to report the offense. Humiliated and embarrassed, they just want to forget it happened.

I did not want to believe racism still exists or that it could happen to me, as if I possessed some super power to avert it. After all, this type of thing happens to other people, but not me. I heard about racial incidents on the national news and read about occurrences in the local newspaper, but I never imagined I would be a victim. I was so wrong.

It happened while I was shopping in an upscale boutique. I was wearing a pair of denim blue jeans, a basic blouse, sneakers, and carrying an oversized purse. Nothing I was wearing screamed name brand. I remember cooler weather, because I wore a hoodie. Immediately upon entering the store, I became the victim of racial profiling. Because I was the only African American in the store, plus the way I was dressed, store workers presumed I was a shoplifter. No one asked me if I needed any assistance, yet I was assigned my own personal escort, unwarranted, to track my every move. I wanted to scream. I wanted to turn and confront my unwanted chaperone, but I just could not bring myself to say anything. I did not want to further feed into other stereotypes by becoming the "angry Black woman," so I left, demoralized. I had the money to purchase what I wanted, but I refused to purchase anything from a business that practices racism of any kind.

Unfortunately, discrimination has existed for centuries. In Luke 10:30–37, Jesus described an incident involving racism. There was a man traveling from Jerusalem to Jericho. The Bible does not mention his race or ethnic background; it simply refers to him as a certain man who embarked on this journey. Jericho was about eighteen miles east of Jerusalem and located in a valley. The trip was a steep and dangerous descent with many curves and hidden places for muggers and robbers to lie in wait for unsuspecting travelers. The road, known as "The Bloody Way," was infested with thieves and treacherous.

Why are we apathetic when we witness blatant acts of racism? Why are we suddenly struck with blindness, deafness, and muteness and refuse to get involved?

This man fell victim to a violent assault. He was brutally beaten, stripped of his clothes, and left for dead. As the man lay on the road wounded and bleeding, a priest approached. No doubt, he saw the victim from afar. Instead of offering assistance, the priest showed no concern for the battered and bruised man and passed by on the other side of the road. He did not even look at the man. He just walked by as if the man were invisible.

Many of us are like the priest and Levite when we witness racial injustice.

Then there was a Levite who saw the man suffering from his wounds and knew he was likely in excruciating pain. Unlike the priest, he approached the man to get a closer look. Surely he would help, but he too passed by on the other side of the road.

Both of these men, laborers in the temple, servants of God, morally upright, pillars of the community, lacked compassion and neglected their moral responsibility to help the man. Clearly, they both saw his dismal condition and chose to ignore his cries.

Why did the priest and Levite refuse to help? Was their refusal to offer assistance out of fear for their own safety? They traveled the same dangerous road. Maybe they were afraid they would suffer the same fate as this man. Perhaps they did not want to get their hands dirty or thought someone else would come along to help. Perhaps they felt it was not their job to help. After all, they worked in the temple and were not physicians. Possibly they thought it would not change anything because the man was half dead anyway.

Many of us are like the priest and Levite when we witness racial injustice. We are afraid of criticism or rejection from our family and peers, afraid of losing our reputation, livelihood, or in some cases, our lives. We may be afraid of losing our position or title in the church. Often we just do not want to get involved or get our hands dirty. It is none of our business. It takes too much time out of our busy schedules to file a police report and maybe testify in court. Let someone else do it. Nothing is going to change anyway.

There was another man who traveled along this dangerous road. In sharp contrast to the priest and Levite, he did not labor in the temple. He was not a servant of God, neither was he well respected in the community. He was a Samaritan, hated and despised because of his race. Nevertheless, he did not allow this to cloud his moral obligation to help the injured man. When he saw him lying on the road in desperate need, he had compassion. He did not wait for another traveler to come along to help. He got involved. He was not concerned about his own safety

Society needs more
Good Samaritans who
can look beyond the
color of skin and
reach across social
disparities to eliminate
discrimination.

or about what others thought of him. He saw someone who needed his help. He did not care about getting his hands dirty. Instead, he showed mercy by bandaging the victim's wounds and taking care of him.

Society needs more Good Samaritans who can look beyond the color of skin and reach across social disparities to eliminate discrimination. Though racism has existed throughout history, our silence allows it to perpetuate. As long as we see nothing, hear nothing, and say nothing, the problem persists.

We can put an end to racial injustice by defending the rights of the oppressed, speaking up for those who have no voice, and showing mercy to the injured. An apology is a great way to start the healing process, but only if it is sincere. Many times people apologize because the camera captured their offense.

Keep the apology; instead, speak out. Say something like the server at a restaurant in Caramel Valley, California, who heard a white guest hurl racial insults at an Asian family. She boldly spoke up against the verbally abusive Silicon Valley entrepreneur and escorted him to the door. This modern day Good Samaritan, unafraid of losing her job, spoke up against injustice.

We must "go, then, and do the same" (Luke 10:37 GNT).

Wisdom Truth

In this new creation life, your nationality makes no difference, or your ethnicity, education, nor economic status—*they matter nothing*. For it is Christ that means everything as he lives in every one of us! (Colossians 3:11 TPT)

Wisdom Prayer

Heavenly Father, thank You for being colorblind and choosing me to be the salt of the earth, a light set upon a hill. Help me not to keep silent when I see injustices, but give me boldness to speak out to upset the social structure of racism. Let me not be fearful of criticism or rejection, but

An apology is a great way to start the healing process, but only if it is sincere.

help me to do what is right in Your eyes. Teach me to show mercy, compassion, and love for others regardless of the color of their skin.

 *Wisdom Reflection*

- How can we demonstrate our moral responsibility to defend the rights of others?
- With the current racial climate, where do we go from here?

_____

_____

_____

_____

_____

_____

_____

_____

_____

Carol Chisolm is a singer and songwriter who suffers with alopecia, an autoimmune disorder that results in hair loss. She coined the phrase, "I have alopecia, but it doesn't have me" to remind her that we are wonderfully and uniquely designed by God and our identity is in Christ and not in a reflection in the mirror. Visit Carol at www.carolchisolm.com.

Chapter Eight

Overcoming
Dr. Grace Allman Burke

My childhood, for the most part, was a happy one. I was the second child of wonderful parents who loved their children immensely. My father, Luther, was a pastor, and my mother, Daisy, a registered nurse. Next to loving God, their three long-awaited children, born somewhat later in their lives, were their greatest joy.

Daisy and Luther had high aspirations for their kids. Achieving a sound education was an overarching goal. They knew, however, the road wouldn't be easy. They had experienced systemic racism in their own educational pursuits. The 1940s through the 1960s, the years they raised they kids, were extremely difficult for Black families pursuing the American Dream.

My parents' fears were realized when I and my siblings entered elementary school. Our teachers were predominantly white, and the student body predominantly African American. The teachers, who didn't live in our neighborhood, made no attempts to understand the background and culture of their students. Their teaching was perfunctory and lacked energy and excitement. In fact, their behavior bespoke unhappy workers who were just doing their jobs, and who couldn't wait for day's end to come. Racial prejudice was rampant among them, as indicated by the need for constant meetings with the principal by my mother, who insisted we receive the grades we earned.

Because of the tenacity of our parents, we learned early to fight for what was ours. We realized we were up against an unfair system and that there were many barriers and ceilings to overcome.

Thankfully, we were taught by our parents that Jesus died for all, and we were included. They showed us in the Bible that all humankind is one, and there are no differences in His eyes. This gave my siblings and me profound courage as we accepted Him as Lord and Savior. As we navigated our educational paths, we were determined to achieve our goals and not give up.

The negative racial incidents I endured during my years of schooling are too many to relate here and were just the beginning of what was to come. I met the same challenges in professional appointments, among colleagues, and in the churches I attended.

I was bypassed for promotions to positions for which I was qualified on several occasions. Only when I challenged the decisions and sought hearings on the matter from higher authorities, was I heard and considered. I then became no longer invisible and a force to be reckoned with.

As an ordained minister, I was asked to officiate at the wedding of one of my white staff members. My credentials were rudely questioned by some of their relatives, and I was asked to show them my license! They refused to accept that I was duly prepared.

When I sought an appointment as an elder in my church after completing my doctor of theology degree, the white associate pastor told me there was no availability. I was then relegated to a lower position, for which there were fewer educational requirements. I accepted the lower position, while awaiting an opening for a higher one. To add insult to injury, a white junior pastor, with fewer credentials and far less experience than I, was appointed my supervisor in the lower position.

Thankfully, we were taught by our parents that Jesus died for all, and we were included.

I was invited by friends to a dinner party in a fancy high-rise apartment building in New York City. When I attempted to enter, the doorman blocked the doorway and advised me the entrance for the "help" was at the back of the building. Of course, I did not comply. After I put him soundly in his place, he backed off and allowed me to enter.

The messages to me were clear: "You are not wanted here." "You're a square peg in a round hole, and you just don't fit." "If I don't acknowledge you, you'll remain invisible, and I can ignore you." Even today, although retired, I still am confronted by variations of this theme. The struggle continues. My children and grandchildren encounter the same messages. I've decided I must teach them the lessons I learned and help them navigate the path to overcoming.

My story is one of victory, despite the brick walls of white privilege, isolation, and marginalization I came up against as an African American woman. How did I overcome? The answer is found in two of my favorite Scriptures: "I press toward the goal for the prize of the upward call of God in Christ Jesus" (Philippians 3:14 NKJV).

The word *press* in this verse denotes the application of force against resistance. Though faced with unspeakable obstacles, the apostle Paul was willing to fight through them because of the high calling on his life. He also had a goal in mind—to achieve a prize from the Lord Jesus for his faithful witness.

With Paul's example in mind, although often discouraged, not once did I back down from the fight. I put my trust in the Holy Spirit, who resides within me, to help me press through the adversities that came my way. It wasn't easy, but, praise God, I am still standing!

Before His crucifixion, Jesus warned His disciples, "These things I have spoken to you, that in Me you might have peace. In the world you will have tribulation: but be of good cheer, I have overcome the world" (John 16:33 NKJV).

I am thankful for the peace that Jesus gives. Although we are engaged in external warfare, isn't it strange that, through Him, we can still experience peace on the inside? When dealing with the insanity of racism, my prayer is always to maintain peace.

I learned how to speak forthrightly, yet dispassionately. A civil rights attorney who helped me fight and win a battle long ago, remarked how much I seemed to

I already had put on the whole armor of God; therefore, I could stand. I was standing, not only for myself, but for generations after me.

be at peace with the situation when the odds were fiercely against me.

In the verse above, Jesus described Himself as an overcomer. By telling His disciples to "be of good cheer," He was letting them know they needed not be discouraged. They had won the battle already, and victory was theirs. That verse gave me much confidence as I faced the many challenges of white supremacy throughout my life. I reminded myself, I am a conqueror through Christ. I am the head, not the tail. I won't take no for an answer.

Another verse that made me stay in the fight is, "If you faint in the day of adversity, your strength is small" (Proverbs 24:10 NKJV). When I was tempted to give up amid a racial skirmish or insult, this verse spoke to me. I got up, dusted myself off, and kept tussling. After all, I already had put on the whole armor of God; therefore, I could stand. I was standing, not only for myself, but for generations after me. A poem by George Banks titled, "What I Live For," expresses it well:

> For the cause that lacks assistance,
> For the wrongs that need resistance,
> For the future in the distance,
> And the good that I can do.[1]

～ Wisdom Truth

Blessed are you when they revile and persecute you, and shall say all kinds of evil against you falsely for My sake. Rejoice and be exceedingly glad, for great is your reward in heaven, for so they persecuted the prophets who were before you. (Matthew 5:11–12 NKJV)

～ Wisdom Prayer

Oh, Lord God, I pray now for my Black sisters who are facing racism and persecution. I pray they will believe deeply in Your love for them and in Your promise to be always with them. Give them courage to endure trials and insults that come their way, not cowering or retreating, but exercising a strong faith in You. Grant them the peace that only You can give—a peace that defies logic or understanding. I pray also for my white sisters. Grant them keen spiritual insight into the racial divide we are still experiencing. Give them practical ideas and plans that will enable them to be active warriors for the truth.

My story is one of victory, despite the brick walls of white privilege, isolation, and marginalization I came up against as an African American woman.

- What decisions will you make in your life to help you be an overcomer?
- Which promises in the Bible will you lean on when the next racist situation confronts you?

_____

_____

_____

_____

_____

_____

_____

_____

_____

_____

_____

_____

Dr. Grace Allman Burke is an award-winning author who has published five books in various genres, including fiction, nonfiction, biblical historical fiction, and a recipe book. She is the 2016 winner of the Christian Literary Awards' Henri and Readers Choice awards for *The Stranger's Son*. Dr. Burke holds degrees in nursing from Cornell and Columbia Universities, and is a retired certified nurse-midwife. An ordained minister, she earned her doctoral degree in theology from Jacksonville Theological Seminary, and she lives with her family in Dallas, Texas. Visit her at graceburkebooks.com.

Chapter Nine

Moving into Freedom
Tonya Williamson

At the start of fourth grade, I was bussed from my mostly Black neighborhood school to a mostly white school across town to be placed in a "gifted and talented" class because my test scores were high. There were no classes like this at the schools near me. I got up extra early to take a long bus ride to school. By the time I got home, it was evening.

I only recall one white student and one white teacher at my old school. The environment was reassuring and welcoming. I liked going to school! I didn't like going to the school I was bussed to. The few Blacks in my class were also bussed. I don't recall any Black teachers, only a Black recess aide who the Black kids gravitated to on the playground and in the lunchroom. Being around other Blacks made me feel like, "You get me, I get you. You like me, I like you." I didn't feel this acceptance at the new school. I just felt bristly, cold interactions that left me feeling like a bother to the thorny teachers.

At the new school, I started questioning my identity, the goodness of people, and my value as a Black person. I didn't feel like I mattered. My teacher was mean—almost hateful—and she showed no empathy, compassion, or motivation to give me what I needed to excel in her classroom. I shrank inward. I thought

> At the new school, I started questioning my identity, the goodness of people, and my value as a Black person.

if I were invisible and stayed out of her way, her thorns wouldn't poke my tender heart. She still found things to pick on me for despite my efforts to disappear from her radar.

The summer before sixth grade, we moved to a white neighborhood. My mom moved us so we could have "better opportunities." She removed me from the school where I attended a gifted and talented class and enrolled me in the elementary school nearest our home.

I missed my old neighborhood. I knew people for blocks surrounding our house because people were sociable and were often seen on their porches hanging out and talking. The few homes that had a garage often left the doors up and people sat inside to socialize. That neighborhood gave me solace. I felt welcome and that I belonged.

People were unfriendly and rarely seen outdoors in the new neighborhood. It seemed they intentionally stayed to themselves. I say this because there were no front porches, no screen doors, and those with garages used them only to enter and exit. There was *no* invitation to socialize! It was a frigid place and I didn't know how to penetrate the iciness.

Bad experiences came with moving to that neighborhood. I no longer fit in with my old friends. They started calling me "Oreo." I was too "white" to fit in with the Blacks and too Black to fit in with the whites. This was devastating. I didn't fit *anywhere*!

Teens had race riots in the neighborhood park. I had to constantly defend myself and my younger brother from white kids wanting to start fights and from berating us using racial slurs. On two occasions, while I was crossing a main street, a car sped up and tried to hit me while someone yelled "Niggerrrr!"

I hadn't experienced such hatred before for being Black. I didn't know how to cope with all the negative experiences. I felt like a dirty penny left on the ground because it had no value.

When I began middle school in seventh grade, the school was about 90 percent white with only one Black special education teacher. I was filled with anger from having so many bad experiences. I didn't like being Black because everything around me said whites were better—they had better things and more things. *Nothing* seemed equal.

Some of my teachers had it in for me. Even though I didn't start trouble, I'd get blamed and be sent to the office. The principal was quick to give me swats and quick to believe I did whatever I was blamed for. Thankfully, the vice principal had compassion. I saw it in his eyes and felt it whenever he smiled at me. His actions planted tiny seeds in my heart that maybe I did matter.

I was raised in church and at a young age learned that Jesus loved me. That, however, only resonated with my head, not my heart. I memorized Scriptures I learned in church to help me cope with the despair I felt. In high school, a Black friend's mother told me I needed to have a relationship with Christ. I had never heard of this before! I spent a lot of time with her learning what it meant.

She taught me to talk to God the way I talked to my best friend. She said to tell God the things I felt, needed, and wanted, and to thank Him for the ways He blessed me. She showed me how to use the Bible as a guide for how to think and live. I did what she said and started applying Scripture to the way I thought and how I treated people.

Throughout my life, I continued to experience prejudice and racism on jobs, in college, and in my everyday life. From studying how Jesus loved hateful people, I learned to love people despite how they treated me. I learned to do good and respond with kindness even when bad things were done to me. Jesus's example taught me to forgive those who spewed hatred toward me. Patterning myself after Christ helped me let go of the anger I felt from the evil prejudice and racism I experienced. When I first learned I was to be like Christ, I failed miserably. I didn't want to be kind or forgiving. Countless times I had to repent for my ungodly reactions to the way I was treated.

I forgave everyone who hurt me. This practice removed the anger and bitterness from my heart. The Holy Spirit taught me to look past stony hearts and prickly people to see what could make them behave the way they did. I discovered hurting people hurt people. If

I was too "white" to fit in with the Blacks and too Black to fit in with the whites.

someone hurts me, something must be hurting them. Christ taught me to look for good in people and to show love.

Now I strive to follow Christ's example. When I encounter prejudice, racism, or injustice, His ways move from the depths of my soul and lead me to love, do good, bless, and pray for people, instead of react in anger. The Holy Spirit transformed me into a completely different person.

At fifty-two, I'm still moving. I recently moved back to the Black neighborhood I moved from and into the house where I spent much of my growing up years. I didn't plan to move back; it was a God-orchestrated move. The move has given me the opportunity to live in the now blighted place my mother moved us from. Some of the same people still live there. I see neglect, despair, and a lack of equality all around me. The relationship I built with Christ has equipped me to handle this environment. Moving back has given me the opportunity to share biblical tools and what I've learned from Christ's example. I've moved from being full of anger, bitterness, and hardly any self-worth, to having love, a God-confidence, and the knowledge that I have great value. I moved from feeling like that valueless penny to knowing I'm a treasure.

Nowadays, regardless of whether I'm surrounded by Blacks or whites, my value doesn't change. I no longer shrink inwardly or feel like I have to defend or protect myself. I *know* I matter. I *know* I have value. I *know* the overcoming, life-giving, protective power of Christ within me. I can confidently stand my ground without having to move from a place of security.

Patterning myself after
Christ helped me let go
of the anger I felt from
the evil prejudice and
racism I experienced.

⌒ *Wisdom Truth*

But to you who are listening I say: Love your enemies, do good to those who hate you, bless those who curse you, and pray for those who mistreat you. (Luke 6:27–28 NIV)

I moved from feeling like that valueless penny to knowing I'm a treasure.

⌒ *Wisdom Prayer*

Lord, life and people can be very difficult. Both can bring much pain. I thank You that You demonstrated how to handle the pain, as well as how to handle prejudice and persecution. Thank You for modeling how to love, serve, do good, and bless people—especially those who mistreat us. Please help us follow Your example. Teach us the right way to handle every situation. Move us along the path of righteousness. Enable us to move in a way that pleases You.

- How have racism, discrimination, or prejudice affected you? How closely have your responses matched Christ's example?
- If you and God had a conversation about these things, what would He tell you to do?
- What are you *willing* to do, and when are you willing to do it?

_____
_____
_____
_____
_____
_____
_____
_____
_____
_____
_____
_____
_____
_____

Tonya Williamson is a Board Certified Biblical Counselor (BCBC), educator, speaker, and writer. She resides in Kansas City, Missouri, with her family. Contact her at Tonyak5777@gmail.com.

Chapter Ten

No Longer a Slave
Christina Custodio

If you are human, and living in the world today, you are probably tired. Some of us feel overwhelmed. Some of us feel hopeless. Some of us feel helpless. Some of us even feel like giving up.

This past year has unearthed a ton of emotions. Many of us had buried these emotions so deep, we believed we would never have to come face to face with them again. We didn't think we could handle it.

I didn't think I could handle it.

I found myself, for the first time, truly addressing the invisible shackles I had been wearing for so long. I finally admitted I was a slave. Not a literal slave, but a slave to negative or faulty thoughts and actions that were holding me captive. Some of my negative thoughts I had inflicted upon myself, and some were forced upon me by others. Regardless of where they came from, I remained in psychological enslavement.

I recently learned from Dr. Paul Tripp, "As human beings, we don't live life based on the facts of our experience, but based on our interpretation of the facts."

I believe this may be why we get so caught up in, then stuck on many of the issues we are dealing with today. It's why we have difficulty acknowledging or believing someone else's interpretation of the facts may be valid. Many of us have become slaves to our own interpretations.

If you too are enslaved by something in your life—an addiction, post-traumatic stress, low self-worth, hopelessness, abuse, negative thoughts, or simply faulty thoughts or interpretations—I have a story for you.

Slaves in the Bible times were different from the slaves brought to America in 1619. Most were closer to the contract workers we have today. They were hard laborers, educators, personal advisors, and they filled all occupational positions. Some became slaves to pay off a debt. By law, they were to be fed, clothed, and sheltered. Some saved up enough money to eventually buy their own freedom.

Now here's the really cool part.

There were many times when a slave became a trusted friend and companion. If he also had a good sense of business, he would be adopted into a family as a son. Under the legal system of that time, sons had permission (power of attorney) to conduct business on their father's behalf.

What? The slave became family. When does that ever happen?

Jesus bought our freedom long ago. It's paid for. So many of us have been walking around in shackles, even though our freedom was purchased a long time ago. We either never knew, forgot, or chose to remain enslaved.

Yes, we have a choice.

Christ not only paid for our freedom, but He also adopted us into His family.

When we choose to be part of God's family, we immediately have access to our inheritance. That includes hope, peace, security, truth, acceptance, love, freedom—and heaven when we are done here.

I feel such joy and excitement as I share with you that there is no condemnation for those who belong to Christ (see Romans 8:1). It's such good news! Although I have known much of the Word all my life, it has been just recently that I realized how much I was allowing to keep me in shackles. I now choose to be free.

Because I've made that choice, my reality has shifted, and I can share that freedom with others. Bible teacher

> Many of us have become slaves to our own interpretations.

Jennie Allen calls it having a "contagious mind."

Today I invite you to choose freedom, become contagious, and change history.

So many of us have been walking around in shackles, even though our freedom was purchased a long time ago.

 *Wisdom Truth*

But when the right time came, God sent his Son, born of a woman, subject to the law. God sent him to buy freedom for us who were slaves to the law, so that he could adopt us as his very own children. And because we are his children, God has sent the Spirit of his Son into our hearts, prompting us to call out, "Abba, Father." Now you are no longer a slave but God's own child. And since you are his child, God has made you his heir. (Galatians 4:4–7 NLT)

 *Wisdom Prayer*

Dear Heavenly Father, You are such a good Father. Thank You for choosing me. You sent Your Son to set me free and have adopted me into Your family. Help me accept freedom from the chains of negativity, lies, and faulty thoughts that often consume my life. Help me step out and away from the shackles You unlocked so long ago through the death of Christ Jesus. Lord, transform my thoughts to reflect who You say I am. I sacrifice them to You today and accept freedom in Christ. Today I stand in Your presence, accepting my place as Your royal child.

- What three lies have you believed about yourself or others?
- Do you have trouble believing you are who God says you are?
- What actions can you take to break free of your chains to change your way of thinking?

_____

_____

_____

_____

_____

_____

_____

_____

_____

_____

_____

_____

Christina Custodio is a wife and mother of three. She is the founder of Agapeland Ministries, dedicated to inspiring women to find joy regardless of their circumstances. She is currently working on a book recounting the forty-four days she lived in a hospital following her son's near death. Visit Christina at christinacustodio.com.

Chapter Eleven

Exclusion Tried, Inclusion Triumphs
Sharon Norris Elliott

As a seventeen-year-old high school senior, honor student, and student body president, I excitedly reported to my guidance counselor's office to discuss my future college ideas. Settling into the tufted leather chair across from the counselor's desk, my heartbeat quickened as I got ready to show the petite, older white woman the catalogs I had been perusing. Over the past six months, I had finally whittled my choices down to five: University of Southern California (USC), Stanford, Spelman, Vassar, and Dartmouth. As I began to talk enthusiastically about why I had chosen these amazing institutes of higher learning as potential places to continue my education, I noticed an awkward nonresponsiveness emanating from the other side of the desk.

The counselor's lips were pressed tightly shut, her eyes a bit squinted, her jaw tight. With her arms crossed, she shook her head back and forth almost imperceptibly, yet enough for me to notice.

"Mrs. Hawkins, what's the problem?"

"Young lady, I'm afraid you've done all this research unnecessarily. Your grades may say you're at the top of your class, but your history as a student of inner-city schools says you are not college material. The rigors of college-level work will simply be over your head. Your hopes will only be dashed when you don't fit in and when you won't be able to do the work."

My forehead wrinkled in both surprise, disbelief, and rising anger. I knew my abilities, the honors and AP courses I had taken, and my rearing in a home where education was a high priority. Both of my parents were university graduates, and my father earned his masters from NYU and his doctorate from California School of Theology.

I also knew my white classmates were not receiving the same "guidance" from this counselor.

My return trip to Mrs. Hawkins's office happened several months later. This time, instead of catalogs, I carried five acceptance letters, fanned out as one would do with playing cards. With the seals of each university clearly showing, I watched as the guidance counselor scanned each seal and each letterhead.

Then I said, "Mrs. Hawkins, I just haven't decided yet."

As a freshman at one of those prestigious universities, I attended the information meeting for sorority rush week. Pledging was high on my list of things to experience in college; however, the girls leading the meeting refused to acknowledge my raised hand. It wasn't until the gathering was almost over that I noticed my skin supplied the only color in the room.

Among further investigation over the following week, I learned from new friends that those white sorority girls had been charged by their mothers' groups not to accept Black girls into their organizations. If they did, their higher-ups threatened not to pay the rent on those beautiful sorority houses.

It was 1975, and I thought I had overcome.

Your grades may say you're at the top of your class, but your history as a student of inner-city schools says you are not college material.

Unlike young people my age who lived in the South, because of my upbringing in Southern California, I had made it to my late teens before I experienced racism. Unfortunately, I learned that my treatment by that high school counselor and those sorority girls were not anomalies. As life continued, the color of my skin caused me to be followed in clothing stores, ignored in car dealerships, and not served in restaurants.

Because of my upbringing in Southern California, I had made it to my late teens before I experienced racism.

But exclusion didn't feel right when I was seventeen, and it has never become acceptable to me. This is America, and according to the Constitution, I am endowed by my Creator with the inalienable rights of life, liberty, and the pursuit of happiness, be that happiness related to joining a service club, buying clothes, test driving cars, or enjoying restaurant meals.

And I was brought up in the church where the Bible teaches me, "There is neither Jew nor Greek, there is neither slave nor free, there is neither male nor female; for you are all one in Christ Jesus" (Galatians 3:28 NKJV). To me, both the Constitution and the Bible scream, "Yes, inclusion is for you," not only as a believer in Christ, but also as a human being in society.

The first chapter in my book *A Woman God Can Bless* is entitled "When Theology and Reality Collide." The context of the verse in Galatians is a conversation discussing the relationship of law and faith. Throughout the chapter, Paul makes the argument that it's not living by the law that makes us right before God, but it's living by faith that does so.

Faith does not discriminate on the basis of race (Jew or Greek), social status (blue-collar or white-collar worker), or gender (male or female). Once we realize how God feels about inclusion, the next verse tells us what our obvious reaction must be: "And if you *are* Christ's, then you are Abraham's seed, and heirs according to the promise" (Galatians 3:29 NKJV, emphasis mine). Since we are one in Christ, we are all heirs of the same incredible inheritance, effectively making us brothers and sisters—the same family.

So is there a connection between the discussion of faith in Galatians 3 and our discussion of racism and inclusion? Indeed. Theology and reality collide. If we believe our heavenly Father meant to have Paul write that men and women of any race and social status are acceptable into the family of God (theology), how dare we exclude family members from anything for those reasons (reality)?

> We are all heirs of the same incredible inheritance, effectively making us brothers and sisters—the same family.

That counselor's attempt at excluding me from receiving my higher education at one of the best schools in the country was the start of my determination to prove, not only personally, but spiritually, that I had the right, the intelligence, and the talent to be represented at any table.

Galatians 3 was only going to be fully realized by doing something about these types of actions, not by ignoring them. Faith without works to make those principles a reality is dead. As I have matured and moved through life, I've come to realize that to live by Galatians 3 myself means speaking up to my white brothers and sisters whenever I see others refusing to live up to the passage themselves.

I realized that we don't know what we don't know. Showing up at "tables" where I normally was not represented became a regular habit. No, I never elbowed my way in, but I never shied away either. When an opportunity presented itself for me to learn something new, have a new experience, or better myself in some way—basically whenever God provided open doors to lead me onward and upward—I was just silly enough to go through them.

Just after writing my first book, when the radio announced a Christian writers' conference was being held at Biola, my alma mater, I registered. It didn't matter to me that the faculty was composed of all white people. Then when asked at the next all-white writers' conference I attended, "How can we change the racial makeup of this event?" my answer was, "Put me on the faculty." They did, and I've been doing my best to blaze that trail ever since.

The same holds true when I'm asked to speak for denominational groups comprised of people who are not my same race. I show up. I freely insert my thoughts, opinions, knowledge, and insight into conversations in which my side of the story has not even been considered. Why is that important? Because we are all "one in Christ." And that oneness demands that my voice be included as equal.

From attempts to exclude me, I have been emboldened to speak Galatians 3 over situations, even to the point of challenging my white brothers and sisters from time to time with suggestions of what can be done to bring about change. I belong at the table in a decision-making, influential, take-me-serious position because I am just like you, made in the image of God, filled with the same Holy Spirit, and one in Christ Jesus.

Heaven is all about inclusion; every race will be there. We may as well get used to that now.

⌁ Wisdom Truth

There is neither Jew nor Greek, there is neither slave nor free, there is neither male nor female; for you are all one in Christ Jesus. (Galatians 3:28 NKJV)

⌁ Wisdom Prayer

Lord, erase our penchant for exclusion, and replace it with a longing for inclusion so we can enjoy the richness of the variety of cultures You have placed in our world.

I belong at the table
in a decision-making,
influential, take-me-
serious position because
I am just like you, made
in the image of God,
filled with the same
Holy Spirit, and one in
Christ Jesus.

- How can you contribute to being sure inclusion takes place in your sphere of influence?

_____

_____

_____

_____

_____

_____

_____

_____

_____

_____

_____

_____

_____

_____

_____

_____

Dr. Sharon Norris Elliott inspires others to "Live significantly!" She's an award-winning author, editor, agent, international engaging speaker, licensed minister, and astute Bible teacher. Author of twelve books (so far), she's associated with AWSA, HSBN.tv, CWWN.tv, ACE, and her own coaching, consulting, editing service, and literary agency, AuthorizeMe.

Chapter Twelve

Love Thy Neighbor
Kennita Williams

I remember the day like it was yesterday. It was 2004, a presidential election year to remember (John Kerry versus George W. Bush), especially since we lived in Florida. I had just started my first "official" position as the assistant to the supervisor of elections, and I was extremely proud and unexplainably excited. As a military spouse I had been overseas traveling with my husband for the previous four years, so this was my time to *shine*! Blue suit, red blouse, pearls around my neck, and my American flag brooch for good measure—I was ready to serve.

Shortly after I arrived at the office at 6:00 a.m., crowds of constituents rolled in behind me. While the voters were being served, I felt like I was being watched. I looked up and noticed a feeble white gentleman standing at the door with his eyes fixed on me. I asked "Sir, can I help you?"

In a loud voice he snapped, "No, you cannot help me." In the same breath he said, "We came a long way from Jim Crow laws, how are you here working the election polls?"

I froze and was at a loss of words. Raised in the North by Bible-believing parents, I and my siblings had been taught to love all people because there is one God and Father of all, who is over all and through all and in all (Ephesians 4:6). I

Raised in the North by Bible-believing parents, I and my siblings had been taught to love all people because there is one God and Father of all, who is over all and through all and in all (Ephesians 4:6). could not believe this man's blatant act of racism.

My boss immediately gave the man the choice to apologize or leave without voting. He stood by his belief and made his choice. With one last glare at me, he turned and exited the building. This man refused to vote if I was handing him his ballot.

While blindsided and disappointed by the man's behavior, watching him make the choice to walk out of the office and not vote made me feel sorry for him. He was holding on to one-hundred-year-old laws that were abolished forty years prior to him entering my office. He was an American standing on American soil who was giving up his right to vote because he refused to see me as an equal. When he walked in that day, he could not see past his prejudice; he only saw the color of my skin.

He didn't know he had encountered a chosen vessel, and a member of God's royal priesthood (1 Peter 2:9). The apostle Paul wrote:

> For he himself is our peace, who has made the two groups one and has destroyed the barrier, the dividing wall of hostility, by setting aside in his flesh the law with its commands and regulations. His purpose was to create in himself one new humanity out of the two, thus making peace. (Ephesians 2:14–15 NIV)

God created each of us on purpose, with a purpose, for a purpose:

> From one man he made all the nations, that they should inhabit the whole earth; and he marked out their appointed times in history and the boundaries of their lands. God did this so that they would seek him and perhaps reach out for him and find him, though he is not far from any one of us. For in him we live and move and

have our being. As some of your own poets have said, "We are his offspring." Therefore since we are God's offspring, we should not think that the divine being is like gold or silver or stone—an image made by human design and skill. (Acts 17:26–29 NIV)

With this in mind, how can we look at our brothers and sisters and tell them they are disqualified because of the color of their skin? We are all God's children, and if we choose racism, we are choosing to disobey God's holy commandment to love our neighbor as ourselves (Matthew 22:39). Paul wrote, "All this is from God, who reconciled us to himself through Christ and gave us the ministry of reconciliation" (2 Corinthians 5:18 NIV). For Christ came to bring reconciliation between us and God, and reconciliation between each other. He came to accept us as we are, whoever we are, "from every tribe and tongue and people and nation" (Revelation 5:9 NASB).

Racism of any kind is wrong in God's eyes, and it should be wrong in the eyes of His sons and daughters. God's love is not restricted to one group or one race and neither should ours be. When Jesus went to the cross, He gave His life for all races and backgrounds. As a Christian my hope is to one day join Him along with *all* of my brothers and sisters who died in Him "from every tribe and language and people and nation" (Revelation 5:9 NASB). We were made in His image, so our lives should be a direct reflection of His life. Love your brother and sister.

Wisdom Truth

So God created man in his own image, in the image of God he created him; male and female he created them. (Genesis 1:27 ESV)

Wisdom Prayer

My Father, thank You for creating me in Your image. I am unique, I am courageous, I am fearfully and wonderfully made,

God's love is not restricted to one group or one race and neither should ours be.

> You have a plan for me
> even when others say
> and see differently.

all by the grace of Your hands. Help me to always remember that it is in You that I live, move, and have my being. Remind me in times of doubt or confusion that You created me for Your use, and You have a plan for me even when others say and see differently. Father help me to love my brothers and sisters as You love them, looking beyond our differences but seeing what binds us together—You.

 Wisdom Reflection

Therefore if anyone is in Christ, he is a new creature; old things are passed away; behold, new things have come. (2 Corinthians 5:17 NASB)

- As new creatures in Christ, how are we to respond to racism?
- How do we as Christians embrace the ministry of reconciliation? (See 2 Corinthians 5:18.)
- Why is it important for Christians to love our brothers and sisters as ourselves?

Kennita Williams is a military spouse, mother of two, and a certified life coach. She has walked a path from not seeing a clear vision to knowing God's purpose for her life. Through her writing she encourages women to be all God has planned for them to be. She's also a qualified addiction specialist for the state of Alaska. She lives in North Pole, Alaska. Connect with Kennita on Facebook and Instagram.

Chapter Thirteen

No Room in the City
Laura Simon

"You're Laura Simon?" she asked as she eyed me warily through the screen door of the leasing office.

"Yes, I am," I said. "It's me. I just spoke to you on the phone ten minutes ago."

The huge smile she had upon hearing my voice while walking to the door had all but disappeared.

I hesitated and spoke again, "You know, I'm the claims adjuster from Allstate?" I said trying to plead my case. I already knew where this was going.

She just stared back at me.

I continued, "The one you just confirmed the appointment with? To see the apartment?" *She remembers me*, I think to myself. I went on, "The one from California?"

And she just stood there, staring at me through the screen door. Not moving, not offering to open the door, and not taking her eyes off my face.

I cleared my throat and asked her again, "Don't you remember me? You do remember speaking with me at lunchtime, yes?"

Then she asked me again, "You're Laura Williams Simon from Allstate? Just moved here from California?"

Again, I tried to smile and softly said, "Yes."

She unlocked the screen door, opened it, and invited me in. "Come this way," she said, as she waved her hand and pointed in the distance. "I'll show you the apartment, but the apartment is no longer available because the tenant has decided to stay," she blurted out while hurriedly walking ahead.

I was almost racing trying to catch up. My heart started beating faster. Now I began praying. More. *What does she mean the apartment isn't available?* Alrighty then. So within the ten minutes it took me to drive here, find a parking space, and walk to the leasing office door, the apartment is now no longer available?

Yeah. Welcome to Metairie, Louisiana, home of the Grand Dragon, David Duke. Yep, Ku Klux Klan David Duke.

This happened a few more times in Metairie before Tony and I finally gave up searching there. We knew we didn't want to stay in New Orleans after housesitting for my sorority sister. The city lit up like a war zone at night, reminding me of the stories I read in history class. Constant shooting all through the night, as well as sounds of police sirens. We went up Highway 10 just a few more miles to Kenner. The city of Kenner had the best mall in the area: The Esplanade. It wasn't as close to my Allstate Building as Metairie, but the traffic wasn't as notorious as California's, so renting there wouldn't be too bad.

But we never got a chance. The leasing managers in Kenner advised us I made more money than they did and that our credit was an issue. Really? We are paying a California mortgage and the rent in Kenner was $375. That was another blow to our young California minds. We never had issues like this back home. My newly-wed husband and I ended up twenty-four miles away in La Place, Louisiana. La Place was far, and we had to cross over Lake Pontchartrain every day. I-10 travels directly over the lake, and there is water on both sides, coming in and going out—scariest thing ever, especially when there is a storm.

Twelve years earlier, in 1993, my husband said, "If there is ever a need to leave the area quickly, we're in trouble. Only one way in, and one way out.

Within the ten minutes it took me to drive here, find a parking space, and walk to the leasing office door, the apartment is now no longer available?

That lake is going to overflow, and we are going to be stuck." When Hurricane Katrina hit, that lake flooded the area and made it hard for the people of New Orleans to escape. With that in mind, we rented a beautiful townhouse in La Place anyway. Tony and I did not have a choice. No one in the city would rent to us. On paper, and over the telephone, we were ideal: the epitome of wonderful potential renters. We were a young Black couple from California with acceptable accents. Everywhere we went, the leasing managers thought we were white.

You make enough money, your credit score is good, and the company you work for is a pillar of the city. Your position in the company allows you to make friends with doctors, lawyers, teachers, pastors, and church leaders and affords exciting opportunities to impact the community. This is fantastic, but there is a problem. You, my dear, are not the right color. This girl isn't in California anymore. Welcome to the South.

Sis, if I may, I would like to speak candidly with you. Racism is very much alive out West, and racism is very much alive in the South. The difference: California runs a covert operation, and Louisiana runs an overt mission. California rents to anyone who has the money. Louisiana does not. In California folks often hide their true beliefs about race under the guise of Christianity. In Louisiana they do not hide their true beliefs, and they use Christianity as a reason to believe what they believe and do what they do. No pretending there whatsoever. None. Zero. What you see and hear is what you get. And you know exactly where you stand. Not so in California.

So what do you do when there is no room in the city? You stop relying on self and lean and depend on God. Not only will He lead and direct your steps, but God may have something bigger and better waiting just for you.

We have read in the Word that God's timing is not our timing, and His ways are not our ways, and He knows what is best for us. I have learned for myself this is true. Tony and I finally went to God about our search. "Where do You want us to live?" we prayed. God led us to a young couple in La Place who had moved into a new and larger home to accommodate their growing family. They already had a

> God showed us what love looks like when people are not concerned about race [and] simply want to be disciples of Christ.

two year old, and Nancy was expecting a baby girl. The new home was less than a mile from the townhouse.

We couldn't believe the miracle God performed! The townhouse had features I had only shared with God from the depths of my heart. It was two stories, two bedrooms, two bathrooms, a huge kitchen with a dining area, and a living room. The Soganas not only rented the townhouse to us for an awesome price but introduced us to the concept of home church, small groups, and marriage ministry.

And did I mention they were white? They brought us in like family. We were the youngest couple and the only Black couple. Their pastor who became our pastor was ninety-two years old, and an awesome man of God. No prejudice. No racism. No judgment. He just wanted to help us prepare for the ministry. His love shown to us erased all the hurt feelings we experienced while searching for a place to live.

Those nine months in Louisiana shaped us, as well as our ministry that was yet to come. Tony and I had no idea we would go back home to California and pastor a church. But that wilderness season taught us so much about people and ourselves. Every white person isn't the enemy, and every Black person isn't a criminal. God showed us what love looks like when people are not concerned about race; simply want to be disciples of Christ; help educate, edify, and encourage the body of Christ; do God's work; share the gospel of Jesus Christ; and spread the love of God.

What shall we do to help each other? Have the hard conversations, share our stories, listen with empathy, and see each other through the eyes of Jesus. I think God would like that.

Wisdom Truth

And we know that all things work together for good to those who love God, to those who are the called according to His purpose. (Romans 8:28 NKJV)

Wisdom Prayer

Father God, I ask You to lead and guide me, and help direct my thoughts and open my heart to other perspectives. Help me see the ways in which I may be blinded about certain issues. Lord, purge my agenda and selfish way of thinking. Help me strengthen my efforts to understand racism and the social injustices that have plagued our country for centuries, and how it has hurt my brothers and sisters of color. Please God, check my heart for any biases or prejudices that may be lingering or hidden, which are not pleasing to You. Lord, I want to live right and do what is right and pleasing in Your sight. Help me to live peaceably with all men.

- Ask God to help you see another perspective.
- Ask yourself if you are part of the problem or part of the solution.
- Have hard conversations and detailed dialogue in your circle of influence.

_____
_____
_____
_____
_____
_____
_____
_____
_____
_____
_____
_____
_____
_____

Laura Simon is an author who sheds light on what it truly means to live a transparent life that honors Christ while staying true to one's self. Experiencing firsthand the societal pressures of being a pastor's wife, Laura writes with an honesty and transparency that breaks boundaries and removes masks. Visit her at lauralsimon.com.

Chapter Fourteen

Strong in Christ
Robyn L. Gobin, PhD

When did you first learn what it means to be a woman? I received my first lesson in the fourth grade on report card day while my mother was reviewing my grades. Having earned straight A's, except for one B, I stood across from my mother beaming with pride, eagerly searching her face for a sign of approval. As her eyes scanned the pink carbon copy paper, her gaze paused in the middle of the page. I could tell something unexpected caught her attention. With displeasure in her eyes, she looked at me and class was in session. "Why did you get a B in science? To survive in this world as a Black woman, you need to be twice as good to go half as far as your peers. I expect better from you."

My mother's lesson that day is not unlike the lessons countless other Black mothers around the country give their daughters. The realities of gender- and race-based discrimination propel them to teach their daughters the importance of being strong Black women—women who are self-sacrificing, emotionally tough, and twice as good as our peers.

There are pros and cons to this concept of womanhood. While our perseverance helps us care for our families, serve our communities, acquire degrees, and achieve career success, we take on too many responsibilities and forget to love ourselves.

We come to believe that self-care is selfish and feel guilty when taking time for ourselves. When we are struggling, we don't ask for help—even if the weight of balancing it all is crushing us on the inside. Our families and communities are depending on us. We don't want to let them down.

Do you believe you have to have it all together all the time?

Do you feel guilty or unproductive when you take time for yourself?

Have you felt pressure to be a strong, confident, and independent woman even when you are hurting on the inside?

Although the world glorifies self-sufficiency, we are not designed to depend on ourselves. God wants to lean in closely and help us navigate the challenges we face as women. When we rely on God, He will strengthen us through the power of the Holy Spirit. In 2 Corinthians 12:9, we are reminded that God's power is made perfect in our *weakness*, not in our strength. But how can we learn to rely on God's strength in a society that's constantly telling us to be self-reliant? There are five habits we can cultivate to depend on Christ for our strength.

1. Prioritize Daily Time with God

Being in a deep and intimate relationship with God is necessary for cultivating the kind of strength that's powered by the Holy Spirit. Spending time with God daily allows us to have the disposition to face everyday challenges, frustrations, and temptations with grace. The direction and answers we seek become available when we get still in the presence of God and listen for His voice. Time spent with God can take on various forms: it could be time spent in His Word through a devotion, listening to praise and worship music, or talking openly and authentically with Him through prayer. The more time we spend with God, the more intimately we come to know Him. It becomes easier to trust that He is more than capable of working within us to accomplish infinitely more than we might ask or imagine (Ephesians 3:20).

To survive in this world as a Black woman, you need to be twice as good to go half as far as your peers.

2. Relinquish Control

God desires us to live free from anxiety and worry. Philippians 4:6–7 assures us of the peace and deliverance we can find in Christ. To experience ultimate freedom and peace, we must be willing to cast our cares on Jesus and relinquish control to Him.

Although the world glorifies self-sufficiency, we are not designed to depend on ourselves.

To relinquish control to Christ, we need open hands (as opposed to clenched fists), a surrendered heart, acknowledgment of our weaknesses, and total reliance on Him. Relinquishing control requires faith. It challenges us to be confident that God is sovereign. We must believe He is capable of meeting our needs and handling whatever burdens we face. When we let go of control, instead of relying on our own understanding and problem-solving abilities, we will wait patiently on the Lord, listen for His promptings, and obey as soon as He provides direction. Much like the cruise control function on a car, when we give God control, we allow Him to guide our decisions, and we trust He will successfully guide us on the path of our purpose (Proverbs 3:5–6; 16:3).

3. Pursue Godly Ambitions

What are you striving to accomplish? Are your ambitions godly or worldly? Worldly ambitions are self-centered and focused on achieving admiration and living up to other people's expectations. God-centered ambitions are focused on using our energy and talents to serve, glorify, and reflect God's light in the world. When we align our ambitions with God's Word, it becomes easier to let go of overworking and people pleasing. Instead of giving of ourselves unto the point of utter depletion, we set boundaries that create more balance in our lives. We release unrealistic expectations. Our focus becomes quality over quantity. We stop depriving ourselves of our own care and attention and begin setting realistic goals, with the sole intent of glorifying God.

4. Stay in Community and Ask for Help

God created us to be in community with one another. When we stay in community with each other, we can share our burdens, lift one another up, and ask for support when we need it. Many of us have learned to suffer in silence when we face challenges and emotional struggles. We've been conditioned to believe asking for help is a sign of weakness and something to be ashamed of.

The truth is, self-reliance is the way of the world. There is no shame in acknowledging your limitations and seeking support from trustworthy, Christlike people. God has commanded us to rely on the support of others by confessing our sins and praying for one another (James 5:16), building each other up (1 Thessalonians 5:11), and spurring one another toward love and good deeds (Hebrews 10:24). We are more effective and powerful together.

5. Replenish Yourself

In today's society busyness and exhaustion are worn like badges of honor. Sis, running yourself into the ground benefits no one. When we don't take care of ourselves, we are more prone to burnout, feeling overwhelmed, and acting without thinking decisions through. You have probably heard the saying "You cannot pour from an empty cup."

Actually, it is possible to pour from a place of emptiness and exhaustion. Many of us (myself included) have been guilty of functioning on three (or less!) hours of sleep, and relying on caffeine to get us through the day. Colossians 3:23–24 instructs us to do everything as if we are serving the Lord. We must ask ourselves, Is pouring from a place of emptiness the type of service that honors God? In 1 Corinthians 6:19–20 the apostle Paul encourages us to view self-care as an act of worship and a way to honor God and commemorate Jesus's sacrifice on the cross. God entrusted us to be good caretakers of our bodies. Self-care is a way

When we align our ambitions with God's Word, it becomes easier to let go of overworking and people pleasing.

that we show gratitude for the body God has given us. When we replenish our-selves through self-care, we are able to show up more fully in service to God, our families, our work, and our communities.

~ Wisdom Truth

> For it is [not your strength, but it is] God who is effectively at work in you, both to will and to work [that is, strengthening, en-ergizing, and creating in you the longing and the ability to ful-fill your purpose] for His good pleasure. (Philippians 2:13 AMP, brackets original)

~ Wisdom Prayer

> *Dear Heavenly Father*, I am at the end of my rope. I need Your strength to sustain me. Help me realize You are the ultimate source of strength. You will never run out or grow weary. Give me the faith, trust, and courage to rely on Your strength as I navigate my responsibilities. Help me remember that self-care is not selfish, but an act of obedience and worship.

There is no shame in acknowledging your limitations and seeking support from trustworthy, Christ-like people.

- How have you been relying on your own strength?
- What do you worry about the most?
- What is one way you can begin to relinquish control to God?
- When your tank is empty, how do you replenish yourself?
- Are the ways you are caring for yourself nourishing your mind, body, and spirit?
- How does the way you take care of yourself glorify God?

_____

_____

_____

_____

_____

_____

_____

_____

_____

_____

_____

_____

Robyn is a wife, dog mom, and psychologist who is passionate about nurturing mental health and self-care among Christian women of color. In her free time, she enjoys trying new recipes, movie nights with her husband, and shopping. You can connect with Robyn on social media at @drrobyngobin or at www.robyngobin.com.

Chapter Fifteen

Finding Hope Again
Chelsi Bennett

"I know this is frustrating," my doctor said as she sat down next to me.

She was absolutely correct. I was frustrated, disappointed, discouraged, and doubtful.

This doctor, my allergist, was the last stop on my ten-plus year tour of specialists, tests, and medications. We had just completed two types of allergy testing, which showed no allergies, and I was devastated. In the last three years, I have had a colonoscopy, endoscopy, abdominal ultrasound, transvaginal ultrasound, taken four classes of insomnia medication, had several blood tests, experienced unexplained pregnancy-like symptoms even though I am on birth control, and have not had a menstrual cycle in a few years, and much more.

This visit was supposed to give me answers on why I could go for days and days feeling nauseous and having stomach cramps that would leave me slumped over in pain for hours. It was supposed to provide me with direction on how to live a normal life without medication. But all the doctor could say was, "There are some diets we can try . . . It *may* be IBS, but I am really not sure."

This news, and not having a clear diagnosis, came on the heels of my gynecologist diagnosing me with adenomyosis. This can only be confirmed and cured via a hysterectomy. The doctor was not making that recommendation yet, just sharing this option. I've endured years of irregular bleeding and cramping, only to be prescribed different types of birth control to minimize the pain and discomfort.

Did I tell you I am only thirty-two years old?

I still remember in high school when lumps of hair started falling out. The doctors had no explanation for it or for the terrible stomach pains that accompanied it. They ran numerous tests and came back with no definitive diagnosis. The only answer they could give was that I must be under a lot stress.

In college I had terrible stomach pains and black, bloody stools. The doctors said, "Let's do a colonoscopy and endoscopy because this sounds like colon cancer or Crohn's disease." The results ruled both out and provided no clear diagnosis for the pain I had been in for years.

This time around Crohn's disease, celiac disease, cancer, pregnancy, and thyroid issues had all been ruled out. After my gastroenterologist did all her tests, I was left with the allergist who, despite my best hopes, had no clear answers.

To be honest, I felt hopeless and worthless. I began to question what was happening in my life and my body. I felt forgotten. As I fell into self-pity, I asked, "Lord, why is it that my diagnoses are rarely clear and certain?"

I know many of you have felt these feelings. You have wondered where God is in the midst of your situation. You have felt alone and maybe even forgotten like I have. I have experienced all those emotions and many more. I have experienced depression and anxiety because I questioned my worth. My health issues have seemed to come back over and over again while I am left with no clear answer for definitive treatment. Let's add frustrated to the list of emotions.

The loss of hope impacted my already shattered self-worth. I have struggled to see Christ's value in me. The numerous health challenges caused me to constantly ask myself, "Why me?" I would look around me at other women who seemed to be thriving and who didn't have to go from doctor to doctor or spend tons of money on co-pays and medical bills.

The only answer they could give was that I must be under a lot stress.

On multiple occasions, I have had to remind myself, "Greater is he that is in you, than he that is in the world" (1 John 4:4 KJV). This Scripture encourages me to recognize my power and authority. It reminds me that I am not alone on this journey—the Greater One is in me. I am confident God created me with a purpose, yet my health has been that thorn to remind me that I need Jesus every step of the way.

I am confident God created me with a purpose, yet my health has been that thorn to remind me that I need Jesus every step of the way.

I have had to preach to myself so I could push my way to the next doctor's visit, or try a new medication, or stand up and present at work when I had barely slept the night before. Those moments have forced me to dig deep into God's strength. In each moment, I had to push through how I felt and what I thought about myself to the place of truths such as these:

> For I know the thoughts that I think toward you, saith the Lord, thoughts of peace, and not of evil, to give you an expected end. (Jeremiah 29:11 KJV)

> The young lions do lack, and suffer hunger: but they that seek the LORD shall not want any good thing. (Psalm 34:10 KJV)

> Be strong and of a good courage, fear not, nor be afraid of them: for the Lord thy God, he it is that doth go with thee; he will not fail thee, nor forsake thee. (Deuteronomy 31:6 KJV)

I have had to place my faith in Christ and not the doctors. My hope has to be in the fact that Jesus is the Great Physician. It would have been easier to only have one medical issue. That isn't my story. It seemed be to issue after issue. I want to know what it feels like to not have to take a medication to fix something that is happening in my body. I want that so much. The truth is, I may experience total healing, or I may not.

I have come to realize that my faith in Christ has to be solely on who He is and not on what I want Him to do for me. Too often we get sidetracked from our purpose in life when troubles arrive and there is no easy fix.

My hope has to be in the fact that Jesus is the Great Physician.

More times than I can count I have lost hope. My saving grace is in three blessings:

1. Community

Having a community that I can reach out to for support—for prayer, words of encouragement, and someone to just listen and vent to—has been vital to finding hope again.

We cannot do this Christian life successfully alone. We cannot be an island unto ourselves and expect to experience all of God's blessings. Be intentional about not being isolated so when you have given your all, you have a tribe of sisters who can pull you back up. God uses people to carry out His purpose in our lives, including blessing us, praying for us, encouraging us, supporting us, and much more. You need women of faith in your life to provide you with practical and spiritual wisdom. This was a struggle for me because it required me to be vulnerable and share my weaknesses and seemingly unanswered prayers with others.

2. Scripture

I sometimes have to muster my remaining strength to find a few words of truth and hope to keep me from doubt and disbelief and despair. Growing up in a Word of Faith church taught me to search the Scriptures so I could quote it and claim it by faith. I have grown in my understanding of hope, faith, and God's sovereignty, yet this practice of standing on the Word has kept me. I know I can stand on God's Word because I have been in many situations where all I had was the Word of God—you know, those late "midnight-hour moments."

3. Purpose

If I am alive with breath in my body, God has a purpose for me. Even in the midst of my pain and anguish, God has something for me to do today. A friend recently reminded me to "trust the process." A few days later, I was venting to my husband about why it has taken over a decade for me to learn it was potentially my diet causing the nausea, insomnia, stomach pains, and body aches. His response was, "It was a process, and you had to go through the process."

Friend, please do not give up. Your burdens are not meant to hold you down but to draw you closer to Christ. When you lose hope, it is okay, but be determined not to stay there. Do not shy away from going through your process and being real about your pain. God is with you. God is for you. The precious Holy Spirit will help get you back to a place of hope and knowing confidently who you are in Christ.

Wisdom Truth

> Now the God of hope fill you with all joy and peace in believing, that ye may abound in hope, through the power of the Holy Ghost. (Romans 15:13 KJV)

Wisdom Prayer

> *Daddy*, be with me today. Help me to see Your hand in the midst of bad news after bad news. Help me to see Your faithfulness even when the burdens seem crushing. Help me to experience Your unconditional love when I feel worthless. Be with me right now in this exact moment.

Your burdens are not meant to hold you down but to draw you closer to Christ.

- What situation has caused you to lose hope?
- What does God's Word say about that situation?
- Who do you have in your corner to hold you up when you are weak?

_____

_____

_____

_____

_____

_____

_____

_____

_____

_____

_____

_____

_____

_____

Chelsi Bennett, JD, is a nondenominational Bible teacher married to a Baptist preacher. She is a former local elected official turned nonprofit lobbyist on a mission to empower women to live out their God-given purpose. The founder of LifewithChelsi.com, the LWC Foundation, CHB Group, and Always Praying Prayer ministry is on social media at @chelsihbennett and online at LifewithChelsi.com.

Chapter Sixteen

My Resting Place
Donna Pryor

I am a mother. I am a Black mother. I am a Black mother who has a son. I am a Black mother who has a son with autism. I am a Black mother who has a Black son with autism. I wish the descriptors didn't matter. I wish I could just say I am a mother who has a son with autism, but I can't. Society won't let me be that. The society we live in makes me look at it in such detail so I can prepare my Black son with autism to face what the world has to offer him—to face the double disability that this country places on boys of color who also have medical conditions that cause them to display atypical behaviors.

It is difficult to teach my Black son "the code" of how to interact with police officers when those trigger behaviors are inherent to who he is. He makes sudden movements, he can't keep still, he makes repetitive movements, he makes loud noises, he doesn't understand shades of gray, only black and white. He won't catch your nonverbal cues or understand your metaphors or colloquial sayings. It is either yes or no. There is no in between. Sometimes and maybe don't exist in his world. Never and always are the concepts he clearly comprehends.

Every time I witness the senseless murder of a Black man by police officers, I think to myself, *If this is the fate of a Black man who knew "the code," and could*

> I can't afford to have my child be his authentic autistic self when he lives in a world where his life has less value than an animal.

understand the verbal and nonverbal cues, what hope is there for my Black son with autism? Would the officer be patient, calm, and unafraid of the color of his skin enough to recognize his autism, or at least recognize him as a human being and not an immediate threat? Would the officer recognize his humanity and consider it before unleashing deadly force?

There is a debate in the autism community about whether parents should have their children go through the various behavior therapies that are available that help teach them to behave in a more typical manner. Some feel we should let them embrace fully their authentic autistic selves—stims, quirks, and all. This may be an option for white parents of white autistic children.

As a Black mother whose Black son is autistic, I don't see this as an option for me. Not in these United States of America. Not when a grown Black man is suffocated for over eight minutes by a police officer while three other police officers look on as if this was routine procedure. We would have seen swifter justice had George Floyd been a dog than a Black man. I can't afford to have my child be his authentic autistic self when he lives in a world where his life has less value than an animal.

The stress of raising a child with special needs can be overwhelming. When you add the extra weight of racial disparities in this country, it significantly increases the burden. When it gets to be too much, when I think I can't take another doctor's appointment, therapy appointment, Individualized Education Plan (IEP) meeting, or meltdown, I go into my resting place.

My resting place is my prayer closet. Yes, it is in my actual closet. In this place I can pray, cry, and complain. I vent. I release all my frustrations right there in that tiny space away from my husband, daughter, and son. This is my safe space. My place of solace and solitude. The place where I don't have to wear the superwife and supermom cape. The place where I can be vulnerable because the One who is there with me knows me best. It is in this place that my soul gets fed and my spirit is refreshed. It is in this place that my dreams are crafted, and my fears are hushed. It is in this place that I find the strength to walk through this world as a Black mother of a Black son with autism and not let the worries of the world drive me to reckless behaviors that would pose a greater threat to my family and my sanity.

It is in this room where I have my daily date with the Divine. Divine Dates is what I like to call what most people refer to as quiet time. This is time I set aside every morning to meet with Jesus and tell Him all about my dreams, fears, troubles, and aspirations. It is where I thank Him for all He has done for me and pray for those who need to know Him. It is my intimate time with the Creator of me!

The One who knew I would be a Black mother of a Black son with autism. The One who knew how long and hard I prayed to be a mother once we received the news that we were infertile. The One who told me, "Come to me, all you who labor and are heavy laden, and I will give you rest" (Matthew 11:28 NKJV). So I show up daily, after my nightly sleep, to let my spirit rest in the presence of God so He can equip me for the day ahead—whatever it may bring. Where He reminds me that "The Lord himself goes before you and will be with you; he will never leave you nor forsake you. Do not be afraid; do not be discouraged" (Deuteronomy 31:8 NIV).

If you don't have an intimate place where you meet Jesus every day, I would encourage you to seek out one. Ask the Holy Spirit to lead you to that spot where you can get still and hear from Him. My spot is a little corner of my closet; yours may be a swing on the porch or the side of the tub in the bathroom. Wherever it is, find it and start having your date with the Divine. He will never stand you up, and He has already paid the bill.

Wisdom Truth

Come to Me, all you who labor and are heavy laden, and I will give you rest. (Matthew 11:28 NKJV)

It is in this place that I find the strength to walk through this world as a Black mother of a Black son with autism.

Wisdom Prayer

Heavenly Father, You alone are the author of our lives. Every day has been penned by You before time began. We look to You for guidance on this journey when life throws us situations and circumstances that feel unfair and unbearable. Strengthen our spirits and renew our minds daily to walk by faith and not by sight. Give us rest in knowing who we are and whose we are, trusting that the plan You have for our lives is one of hope and a future.

Wisdom Reflection

What have you been wrestling with on your own that you need to bring into your resting place? Ask the Holy Spirit to show you a Scripture that speaks to that issue. Meditate on it. Rest in it and listen for God to guide you through the darkness and into His marvelous light.

_____

_____

_____

_____

_____

_____

Donna Pryor is the author of the marriage devotional *Bone of My Bones and Flesh of My Flesh*. She and her husband, Charles, founded the Pryor Experience Group, whose mission is "Keeping Couples Connected So Families Thrive." Visit her at thepryorexperiencegroup.com.

Chapter Seventeen

He Heals the Brokenhearted
Kenya Edwards

The human heart is an organ made of muscle, housed in my chest cavity, and located on the left side just behind my breastplate. Although I know how strong my heart is and the work it does to sustain life for me, there was a time when I felt like my heart was breaking. Impossible? How can something that sustains a human being break? How *can* an organ that never stops pumping good blood through our bodies become so tender when pierced and so fragile when taken for granted?

My conscious mind knows a heart cannot literally break, but it can certainly feel as though it has. It can happen in the blink of an eye. One minute you are on top of the world. You feel all is well, and that nothing in life could be as precious as it is at that moment. Then, suddenly, it all changes. An indescribable pain comes when a life-changing experience shatters your every thought of normalcy.

The instant your heart encounters that stressful event even has a medical term—it is known in the world of science as broken heart syndrome.

I just know when it happens, life is never the same.

It could be the pain you experience from the loss of a loved one, the pangs you feel when a child has gone astray, or the despair you feel from the end of a

How wonderful it is to
know that the God of
all creation is the glue
that puts us together
again.

relationship. All these things can cause a heart to ache.

I had the opportunity to become acquainted with this "broken heart syndrome" firsthand. My heart-shattering moment occurred when I realized I would no longer be in a union that I thought was for life. I was going through a divorce. It was as if my heart cracked, shattered, and crumbled into multiple pieces. I felt as though all the issues of life that had been held in my heart, all my secrets, all my fears, all my disappointments were now spewed out for all to see. No glue in the world could ever fix it. What was I going to do?

It was in that very moment I realized that God was closest to me.

God's Word tells us, "He heals the brokenhearted and binds up their wounds" (Psalm 147:3 NKJV). Jesus sees your hurt; He feels your pain. Isn't this also the reason that Jesus came? When Jesus came it was for more than just to grant us access back to the Father through salvation. He did not only come to heal the sick and feed the poor or to give us life more abundantly. He came to be touched with all our infirmities, to fully understand what we feel and experience daily.

How wonderful it is to know that the God of all creation is the glue that puts us together again.

Psalm 34:18 tells us the Lord is close to those who have a broken heart. With over thirty references in the Bible pertaining to broken hearts, it leads me to believe the heart can and does break—and when it breaks it can also be restored.

To allow God to fully restore us back to wholeness, we must find out the real root of our brokenness. What is the cause of our broken hearts? Why do we suffer so much pain when we get our feelings hurt?

Could one of the causes be that we harbor unfulfilled expectations? Can it be misguided trust in man above God? Or could it be our own pride?

As humans, we are always looking for someone or something to satisfy our needs, whether it's a new car, dress, house, or career. We look to fill the void in our lives with materialistic items, objects that can never satisfy.

Life has taught me there is only One who can fill any void that I might have in my life—and more importantly in my heart—and He is my Lord and Savior, Jesus Christ.

When we are most vulnerable, we should seek the love of our God. Instead of having a "Why God? Why?" party, we need to look toward the Lord, where our help comes from. He loved us before He created the heavens and the earth. He loved us before we were formed. He loves us through our brokenness and guilt. He simply and purely loves us. His love is the catalyst that sent His Son Jesus.

"For God so loved the world that He gave His only begotten Son, that whoever believes in Him should not perish but have everlasting life" (John 3:16 NKJV).

With all this love surrounding us, we should seek God's wisdom on how to fill the empty spaces in our hearts. With all this love we should be looking only toward the One who has our best interests in mind. Why haven't we done that? We become so consumed with the flow of life that we forget to seek the One for whom we were created. We take for granted the blessings that we receive as being part of everyday life, and we became ungrateful.

But all is not lost, there is an answer to all that we seek.

His name is Jesus. Jesus is the person of the Trinity who stepped down from His heavenly place to walk among us. Jesus came as a man not to be served but to serve. Jesus is the Son of God, the One who laid down His life so we could have life eternal. Jesus is the Prince of Peace.

There is an indescribable peace that only He can fill you with when you are broken or feeling unworthy. The peace that I am talking about floods in like the tide from the ocean, gently covering us with its strength, while washing away the guilt, shame, anger, disappointments, and the emptiness we feel when our hearts are broken.

The prophet Isaiah reminds us that God will keep us in perfect peace when we keep our minds focused on Him. Keep your focus upon the Lord, no matter how the situation looks. Jesus understands and is touched by what we feel and experience since He walked this earth as a man. God is with us and for us in all situations, and He will never leave us or forsake us.

Life has taught me there is only One who can fill any void that I might have in my life—and more importantly in my heart—and He is my Lord and Savior, Jesus Christ.

Wisdom Truth

The Lord is close to the brokenhearted and saves those who are crushed in spirit. (Psalm 34:18 NIV)

Wisdom Prayer

Lord God, in the name of Your Son Jesus, I give You all the praise, all the honor, and all the glory that is due to You. There is no other God before You, and there will not be any other after You. As I stand before You broken, wounded, hurt, and uncertain, I ask for Your peace to cover me in my pain. I ask for Your guidance amid the trials and challenges that I face every day. I know You walk with me in all I do. Although I am in a low place at this moment, help me understand the test, so I will not have to repeat it. But, if I should have to repeat it, I know You will be with me again to guide me through. Teach me Lord to wait on You and to follow Your steps. Teach me to be still, so I will see You are always there, You are always merciful, and You are always full of grace.

We become so consumed with the flow of life that we forget to seek the One for whom we were created.

- What do you do when you are feeling lost and hurt?
- Do you turn to God for guidance?
- Do you feel that God hears you when you call to Him?

Kenya (Kay) Edwards is the producer and host of the talk show "What Would Kay Say?" on Radio Free Brooklyn. She holds a master's degree in psychology with an emphasis in life coaching. You can find her at radio freebrooklyn.com, Instagram/wwkaysaytoday, Instagram/hisapparel, and Facebook/officialHisApparel.

Chapter Eighteen

Adopted by Two Fathers
Rosemary Norris-Skates

I heard Auntie say, "Ophelia is more her Auntie than me."

I heard it; it caught my attention, but I dared not inquire. I had heard her make that comment more than once but kept my thoughts and questions to myself. It was something I probably wasn't supposed to hear. Children were to be seen and not heard back then, and they never had an opinion.

One morning I woke up after having a dream I don't remember anymore; but whatever it was, it prompted me to ask Mommy if I had brothers and sisters. She quickly changed the subject. All my friends had siblings, and although they had fights among themselves, they always joined forces when things happened to them. I didn't have anyone to side with me, and I felt alone. I always felt there was something missing, but I could never figure out what the something was.

I was full of fear and anxiety much of the time but didn't really know about what or why. I struggled in school. I wasn't particularly smart or popular; in fact, I felt almost invisible. I was there but not noticed. Math was difficult, science was foreign, and the rest was like the adults talking in the Charlie Brown movies, just meaningless noise.

Daddy's brother and his wife, Uncle Thom and Aunt Frances, were in my life when we lived in Cleveland, and their kids were my cousins, but I *knew* I was not their sister even though we had the same last name. Daddy would take me to their house most weekends. I was never mistreated, but the strong sense of not belonging was constantly with me.

Daddy was an absentee father. His clothes were there, but he was gone most of the time. When he was there, it was only because he was getting ready to go someplace and needed a change of clothes. We didn't have family time; we just shared the same address, but that was the extent of it.

Mommy and I moved to Memphis when I was almost ten years old. When I was sixteen, I was told I was adopted. I was shocked to learn that Mommy was not my "real" mother, but Daddy was my real father. After some back and forth Q and A, I finally got an answer to the gnawing question that had haunted me for years: Yes, I did have brothers and sisters.

I always knew something was missing, and the aha moment had finally come. After years of wondering, I asked "the question" and finally got a straight answer. Because of what I called my "homing device," which I believe all adoptees have, deep inside I knew something was missing. Although I had been with the people I knew as my parents all of my life, I also was aquatinted with my biological mother, but never knew she was my mother. I had played with my siblings when I was a young child, and thought my sister was my cousin. I came up with this in my child's mind because her grandfather was married to my aunt, Daddy's sister.

Years later, I have come to understand the significance of adoption and the importance it holds. Unfortunately, many people who are adopted never realize how special they are. As a born-again believer, I came across the term "adopted" in the Bible. By this time, not only was I adopted, but my two children were also adopted by my husband, who was not their natural father.

I always felt there was something missing, but I could never figure out what the something was.

Since it seemed to be a reoccurring theme running through my life, I took a genuine interest in learning what it meant to be adopted. I realized adoption is not only biblical, but it is also honorable. I learned that God, our heavenly

Father, also adopted His children. I was pleased to find that I was adopted twice, by my biological father and my heavenly Father. I was excited to know this, and I now had a valid response to those old self-defeating thoughts. No matter how they made me feel, I could remind myself I was a child of the Most High God. Rejection no longer had the same power over me. I learned that God decided to adopt me into His family. When I understood who I was and whose I was, my whole attitude about life changed.

Unfortunately, many people who are adopted never realize how special they are.

The decision by my mother to give me to my natural father may have been a good choice, but the spirit of rejection kept reminding me that she rejected and abandoned me. This made me feel I was an inconvenience to everyone. That all proved to be a lie because I now know I was loved and wanted from day one. I came to understand it was simply best for me and everyone involved under the circumstances I was born into.

The best part is I had the opportunity to know my daddy and his family. I was later reconnected with my birth mother and her family. With open arms I was accepted into the part of my family I didn't know. I feel I have had the best of both worlds.

Adoption can make a person feel displaced, unnecessary, inadequate, and insignificant. I felt all of those things at one time or another. However, when I gave my heart and life to Jesus, I began to see how valued and necessary I really was. Because of my circumstances I was especially interested in the details of adoption and the spiritual implications. Finding I was adopted into the family of God, in addition to my natural adoption, I realized I am an heir of God. Since I am an heir, I have an inheritance.

When Daddy and Mommy adopted me, the inheritance I received was my father's name and access to his family. All that he had, I inherited. I had the right to receive what and who he was, and all he possessed, naturally and spiritually. There were mountains to climb and much to overcome, but I did.

Daddy's father was a minister, and I inherited that. I was born again and Spirit filled in September of 1977. To my knowledge there are two of his granddaughters who are ministers—my cousin and me. The fact that I am adopted by both my

> Adoption can make a person feel displaced, unnecessary, inadequate, and insignificant. I felt all of those things at one time or another.

natural father and my heavenly Father validates everything about me as a child of God and now as a Christian woman.

What the devil meant for evil, God has used for my good. My beginning may have been unsettling and filled with uncertainty, but now I know who I am and to whom I belong. I understand my significance, my adequacy and sufficiency in Him. I am able to do all He called me to do. I am blessed to be the daughter of two adoptive fathers, the Most High God and my Daddy.

The Scripture that speaks to me and keeps me grounded when I have mental battles is, "To the praise of the glory of His grace, by which He made us accepted in the Beloved" (Ephesians 1:6 NKJV). The one word in this verse that excites me most is *accepted*. I have been accepted by God Almighty, with all of my flaws and faults. God's acceptance overrules the spirits of rejection and abandonment.

During the times I struggle with knowing about myself and my shortcomings, there is consolation in God's Word. "For I am confident of this very thing, that He who began a good work in you will perfect it until the day of Christ Jesus" (Philippians 1:6 NASB). I know God is not finished with me. He is working on me, molding and making me into the woman He called me to be.

It's up to me to believe Him over my finite thoughts and false opinions. I know I am not alone. The Word of God is true. There is no hiding from His powerful, piercing Word. It meets me where I am and exposes my thoughts and the intents of my heart. I now understand my heart is open and naked before Him, so I must be honest when I pray. When I am afraid, disappointed, hurt, or angry, it is useless to pretend I'm not. The liberating truth for me is He wants me to come to Him honestly and broken, trusting Him to heal and make me whole—spirit, soul, and body.

To the praise of the glory of His grace, by which He made us accepted in the Beloved. (Ephesians 1:6 NKJV)

Father, You are all wise and all knowing. You have made me, and others like me who have been adopted, very special. Thank You for allowing me to come to know and understand that adoption is Your idea, and parents who adopt have done a good thing. Help each adopter and adoptee realize how wonderful they are, but more so, how marvelous You are.

My beginning may have been unsettling and filled with uncertainty, but now I know who I am and to whom I belong.

- When you are dealing with issues you need to overcome, what do you do?
- When you are feeling hurt, rejected, and unloved, who do you turn to?
- The Scriptures that were written to the churches are written to you and me. Replace the word *you* with *me* and make it personal.

_____

_____

_____

_____

_____

_____

_____

_____

_____

_____

_____

_____

Rosemary Norris-Skates is an ordained minister, mentor, and certified counselor. She discovered as a teen she was adopted, and that knowledge led her to receive Jesus Christ. Rosemary is a devoted wife, mother, grandmother, and great-grandmother.

Chapter Nineteen

Overcoming in Challenging Times
Brenna J. Fields

Over the last three years, I have experienced an extended season of overcoming. Dictionary.com defines the word *overcome* as "to get the better of in a struggle or conflict; conquer; defeat: to overcome the enemy; to prevail over (opposition, a debility, temptations, etc.); surmount."

One of the first ideas that comes to mind about overcoming is that something has occurred to cause us to need to rise above it. Something has happened to overwhelm us, and we may feel crushed or even defeated by it. But when we overcome something, we conquer it, we subdue it, and we are victorious over it.

As I share these words, this season in my life has come to an end. Thank you, God! I am now able to reflect on it so I can glean its life lessons. One of the lessons I've learned is how to overcome in challenging times. I am sharing my story with you in the hopes that, as you experience life challenges, you can use the lessons I have learned and overcome just as I have.

During this period of time, my family experienced the loss of eight family members, including the women in my family who were my mother figures. My godmother (in Louisiana culture, we call her Nanny or Nanan), my mother, and my grandmother have all made their transitions to their heavenly home.

As soon as our family began to catch our breath after losing one person, the phone rang again to inform us of the loss of someone else.

It seems as if our family blinked, and they were all gone. In between those deaths were the passing of cousins and an uncle. Some deaths were after a long illness, and some were very sudden and tragic. As soon as our family began to catch our breath after losing one person, the phone rang again to inform us of the loss of someone else. And in this midst of all of this, I lost a close friend very suddenly. It was an overwhelming time.

In addition to my grief, I made the difficult decision to file for divorce, to leave a marriage that was verbally, emotionally, and mentally abusive. Once the divorce process began, the abusive behavior continued, and even escalated, with threats to "expose me for the person I really was," blaming me for the deaths of all of my family members and threatening to take everything that belonged to me.

My faith was my saving grace in overcoming all of these tragedies and challenges. Each of the things that happened were because we live in a fallen world. God did not intend for man to die, but because of the sin of our original parents Adam and Eve, each of us will experience physical death. God also did not intend for husband and wife to behave abusively toward each other, but sadly, this is a reality in some marriages (again, pointing back to sin).

A passage in 1 John 5 gives us insight into how we can overcome the world and its fallen nature—we overcome by faith. In his commentary on 1 John 5, Matthew Henry says:

> Faith is the cause of victory, the means, the instrument, the spiritual armor by which we overcome. In and by faith we cleave to Christ, in contempt of, and in opposition to the world. . . . It has the indwelling Spirit of grace, which is greater than he who dwells in the world.[2]

The first lesson I've learned about overcoming by faith is to, as Matthew Henry stated it, "cleave to Christ." Cleaving to Christ means to lean into Him and His

Word, believing it to be true, not just in general terms, but true specifically for our individual situations.

As I faced the very sudden death of my mother, I gained comfort in knowing I could learn from biblical characters who also experienced great loss and grief. In Job 30:27–28 (NKJV), Job said, "My heart is in turmoil and cannot rest; days of affliction confront me. I go about mourning, but not in the sun; I stand up in the assembly and cry out for help."

In reading Job's story, I was comforted to know God never left Job while he was struggling, and that He would eventually show Himself to Job and restore him. For me, cleaving to Christ meant He never left me and He would restore me, even though there were times when God seemed to be silent with me. Cleaving to Christ also meant I could tap into His wisdom to navigate what I was experiencing. Lastly, cleaving to Christ meant I would try to live my life as He did—forgiving those who mistreated me and not desiring vengeance from my own hand. As we cleave to Christ, we overcome by faith.

The second lesson I learned is grace has a role to play in our overcoming by faith. What is grace? Grace can be defined as unmerited favor. It is something that we are gifted with, not because we deserve it, but because of how God loves us. We cannot earn grace; we receive it because of who God is.

Mary Fairchild gives us a definition of grace as "a special virtue, gift, or help given to a person by God."[3] As believers in Christ, the Holy Spirit is a gift living inside us who enables us to overcome. We cannot conquer, survive, or thrive in our own strength and power. God's grace provides exactly what we need to endure, to withstand, and ultimately to win. Jesus reminds us of our dependence on Him: "Yes, I am the vine; you are the branches. Those who remain in me, and I in them, will produce much fruit. For apart from me you can do nothing" (John 15:5 NLT). As believers we have exactly what we need to overcome, as long as we stay connected to the Vine. We remain connected to Jesus Christ and receive His grace to overcome by faith.

As I faced the very sudden death of my mother, I gained comfort in knowing I could learn from biblical characters who also experienced great loss and grief.

Third, I've learned that overcoming by faith means there is a battle to be fought. As we face challenges and rely on the power of God to help us, we are engaged in spiritual warfare. Ephesians 6 teaches us about the weapons available to us (both defensive and offensive) to help us as we strive to triumph over life's challenges. When we overcome in Christ, we can be confident in knowing that, ultimately, the victory is ours. We trust God to give us the victory and also believe that our victory will be exactly what we need, not necessarily what we may think it should be.

God is sovereign and omniscient; God is omnipresent and omnipotent. He is able to orchestrate people, things, and conditions so they turn out in our favor for our victory. As we engage in spiritual warfare, we are trusting God that we will win and overcome by faith.

In 2020, the world experienced a global pandemic (COVID-19). In addition, our country faced racial unrest not seen in over fifty years.

Whether our struggles are global or personal, I believe we can use the same lessons I shared in overcoming them. We can cleave to Christ and allow Him to guide us in this season, we can depend on God's grace to give us what we need, and we can engage in spiritual warfare and trust God. We do not know when our global and personal challenges will come to an end or how they will be resolved, but we have our faith. Our faith is how we endure and how we overcome. By faith we watch God work in our lives for our good, for our victory, and for His glory. Praise God! By faith, I am an overcomer.

As believers in Christ, the Holy Spirit is a gift living inside us who enables us to overcome.

Wisdom Truth

For whatever is born of God overcomes the world. And this is the victory that has overcome the world—our faith. Who is he who overcomes the world, but he who believes that Jesus is the Son of God? (1 John 5:4–5 NLT)

Wisdom Prayer

Father God, thank You for being a faithful and loving God who is always there for us. Thank You for reminding us that whatever is born of You overcomes the world. Because we believe in Your Son Jesus Christ, we can overcome the world. Help us to walk in our victory by faith. Help us trust You in this season of life's challenges, knowing we will be victorious, that things are working for our good, and that You will be glorified in and through us. We are excited about what our future in You holds. Thank You, God, that we are overcoming by faith.

We trust God to give us the victory and also believe that our victory will be exactly what we need, not necessarily what we may think it should be.

Wisdom Reflection

- What are some things you can do to "cleave to Christ" in your season of overcoming?
- How has God helped you overcome life challenges in the past?
- What spiritual lessons can you learn from your past that can be applied to help you overcome now, as well as someone else?

Brenna J. Fields is an ordained minister, entrepreneur, writer, and certified life coach (New Season, New Day Coaching and Mentoring) who desires to help women experiencing life challenges to live fulfilling lives so they can then pour into the lives of others. She can be reached at newseason newday.com.

Chapter Twenty

Leap of Faith
LaShondria M. Smith

In spite of it all, I did it! I got four people on a plane. This was my goal as my mother-in-law received her ultimate healing from cancer, leaving us on March 19, 2015.

Burned out from work, church, family, and just life led me to seek God for something different. My husband, Willie, and our two younger sons, Dorian and Donterrio, took a "leap of faith" in heading to Adana, Turkey, to advance my career and partake in European living, or so we thought. We PCS'ed (permanent change of station in military terms), leaving our older two sons, Darren in South Carolina to work and LaDareon in Georgia to finish his senior year of college. Everyone thought we may have lost our minds, but I knew what the Lord said, and I trusted Him and His plan.

Our family has always been active in our local church and community. Willie and I both were leading ministries. Willie had partnerships with the county high schools to photograph sports, something he truly loved doing. The boys were thriving and growing academically as well as partaking in sports and other high school activities. I held a leadership role in the local chapter of my sorority and served as a youth leader leading weekly Bible studies and helping youth prepare for life after high school.

Life was good for us, and we thought Georgia would be home forever, but God had another plan. Proverbs 19:21 (NLT) says, "You can make many plans, but the Lord's purpose will prevail." This became real to us as we prepared to leave everything that was familiar and tread into new waters. There are times in our lives when we have to want what God wants for us because He knows what is best.

At the beginning of 2015, I decided to seek God through a seven-day fast for something different, a change. The Friday prior to the Martin Luther King Jr. holiday weekend, I interviewed for a promotion; by mid-February the job offer came. With Willie's support, I accepted. *Yes, Lord, this truly is something different, leaving our older sons Stateside, trusting You to take care of them, heading across the world to a foreign place.*

"Trust in the Lord with all your heart and lean not on your own understanding; in all your ways submit to him, and he will make your paths straight," says Proverbs 3:5–6 (NIV). We would have to trust the Lord and walk on the path He was leading. This was a place of surrender and letting go of my plans and what I wanted, and walking in what God had ordained for my life.

I recall a date night Willie and I had prior to leaving. While walking to the car after dinner, I looked up into the sky and saw a crescent moon with a single star beside it, the symbol of the Turkish flag. Tears welled up in my eyes as the Lord confirmed it was time for something different and that we were walking in obedience.

Oh, did God make our paths straight! Oftentimes in Black families, we become enmeshed with our extended families and do not truly leave and cleave in uniting with our spouse. "For this cause shall a man leave his father and mother and cleave to his wife" (Mark 10:7 KJV). In this new place, God truly established our marriage and family in His way. Even though Willie and I had been married twelve years, in Turkey we learned how to depend upon each other and grow together as husband and wife.

> There are times in our lives when we have to want what God wants for us because He knows what is best.

Our sons matured and came into their own, even the older two back home. Willie gained his first civilian position after being retired from the U.S. Air Force for seven years, and his photography business grew by leaps and bounds. Professionally, I became a leader, developed others, and gained recognition for the success of my programs.

"Lord, why are You breaking up our family?" I asked. He reminded me, *You took a leap of faith. Where is your faith now? Trust Me.*

We connected with liked-minded people who became lifelong friends. I returned to music ministry, leading worship in this dry place. Spiritually it was fertile ground for God to increase my faith and use me to minister to His people. I finally walked in total obedience and began a women's Bible study. The ladies were excited, had a hunger for God's Word, and yearned to know how to apply it to their lives. God was doing a mighty work and it could only get better, or so I thought.

Due to turbulent times in Turkey threatening our safety, Willie and the boys were ordered to depart and head to Germany to finish up the school year without me. We were devastated. It was as if God had finally brought us to a place of oneness, where we were growing as a family and in our professions, and now we faced a separation. This made no sense. This was difficult because I had never been away from our boys. It had been years since Willie was deployed, leaving me alone.

"Lord, why are You breaking up our family?" I asked. He reminded me, *You took a leap of faith. Where is your faith now? Trust Me.* Hebrews 11:1 (KJV) says, "Now faith is the substance of things hoped for, the evidence of things not seen."

After they left, I continued the Bible study as it offered a place for the ladies and me to find strength, hope, and encouragement as we learned to survive without our families. We were desperate, walking by faith, seeking the Lord, trusting His plan. Worship at the one contemporary service each Sunday at the chapel went to new heights and deeper depths as we united with our brothers and sisters of different nationalities. His presence filled the chapel weekly, and lives were being transformed. It was a glimpse of how all God's people would one day come together in heaven.

Although God was showing Himself, using me for His glory, and teaching me how to trust Him, I missed my family. I recall one day after work I was watching *Family Feud* while sweeping, not usual for me at all as we had a housekeeper. I looked out of the back door into a beautiful sunset and said to the Lord, "You left me, You forgot about me." I began to weep and lay on the sofa until I cried myself to sleep.

The following day, my commander walked into my building and frantically asked me, "Where do you want to go?"

This was a no-brainer, and I said, "Anywhere my family and I can be together."

"I'll work on it," he said.

"Sir, why am I a priority now?"

He told me he had been in a meeting the previous night at the Air Force Personnel Center and the Senior Executive Service (SES) civilian mentioned my name during the meeting and requested the commanders do all they could to get me out of Turkey.

"And the Lord said to Moses, 'I will do the very thing you have asked, because I am pleased with you and I know you by name'" (Exodus 33:17 NIV). My God had not forgotten about me! Although lonely without my family, I had stayed faithful and walked in obedience.

My commander asked, "Do you know the SES?"

"No, I don't."

He looked surprised and said, "But she knows your name."

I replied, "That is the Lord who heard my cry. And He knows my name."

Worship at the one contemporary service each Sunday at the chapel went to new heights and deeper depths as we united with our brothers and sisters of different nationalities.

God loves me so much that a senior leader whom I had never met said my name and requested a new assignment for me.

My Turkey experience increased my faith like never before. God showed me how to trust Him even when I did not see or know how He would work it all out by making a way for my family and I to reunite.

Trust in the Lord with all your heart and lean not on your own understanding; in all your ways submit to him, and he will make your paths straight. (Proverbs 3:5–6 NIV)

~ Wisdom Prayer

God, You created me, You know my name, and every fiber of my being. You will never leave me nor forsake me. Please forgive me for the times I did not trust You and questioned Your plan. Help me to keep my heart open to Your perfect will for my life because You know what is best for me. God, You are faithful and always make a way. Thank You, God, for just being God.

God showed me how to trust Him even when I did not see or know how He would work it all out.

- In what areas of your life do you need to trust God more?
- Take a moment to write those down. Now submit them to God by asking Him to open your heart to trust Him and His plan.

LaShondria Smith is the Founder of *Legacy of Hope, International,* a non-profit organization centered in community care. Her desire is to make an impact in the kingdom of God by helping women and girls find their identity in Christ and walk in purpose. You can find her on Facebook.

Chapter Twenty-One

Because His Blood Was Red

Jamila Jenkins

I have never felt the need to question, defend, or apologize for who I am. My truth is when I go to bed at night, I'm Black, and when I awake in the morning, I'm Black. I'm always Black. It is the one thing I cannot change, deny, or cover up, it just is. It is also the thing that I love about me.

I wear many hats. I'm a wife, mother, daughter, sister, friend, pastor, entrepreneur, life coach, author, creative, mentor, academic, and several other things that characterize me. I'm also a corporate employee for a large healthcare company (or conglomerate, depending on how one looks at it). You'd never know I'm any of the roles I fill or walk in without my making mention of it or someone seeing me in action. Some of these roles come with uniforms that are interchangeable and overlapping, but none of them define me as a Black woman.

For most of my life, being Black or African American was a non-issue. I grew up in a community (or village as my grandmother would say) of people who looked like me, spoke like me, and had dreams and aspirations that were similar to mine. It wasn't until college I learned the depths of difference and experienced culture shock that shook me to my core. For as much as I knew my community, it was not the full representation of the world; it was what I knew and had grown accustomed to.

My truth is when I go to bed at night, I'm Black, and when I awake in the morning, I'm Black. I'm always Black.

As I met people and grew comfortable in my new surroundings, I was able to relax. But then incidences like those I saw on the Sunday Night Movie began to occur.

I had a car accident on campus where I was hit by another student. She waved me out, giving me the okay to make a left turn, or so I thought. But then she proceeded to accelerate and ran directly into my driver's side door. I was devastated and remembered thinking, *This can't be life*. I was given a citation for failure to grant the right of way.

I've never been one to pull the race card, but I immediately thought how wrong this whole incident was and attributed it to being Black. I thought of the many times in Black history where the Black person had to give access or credence to a white person; when they didn't, they were cited with failure to grant superiority (the *right* of way).

The other driver was a white student who offered me the "go" but then rescinded it after hitting me. The icing on the cake was she had no insurance. I guess God was building my tolerance muscles.

I was nineteen at the time and had never really experienced racial discrimination. I decided the best way to combat it was with education. I took courses on race relations, African American studies, communication, and any other course that would affirm me in my skin. The more I immersed myself in social studies and race relations topics, the more experiences I seemed to have. I was becoming hyperaware of things that had not bothered me before—perhaps because my focus shifted from living to validating my existence.

We live in a time now when many people are struggling to separate facts from feelings and reality from illusion. Discrimination is everywhere and can be scarily disheartening. My melanin enters the room before my character does and is followed by my personality. Unfortunately, the depth of my skin color speaks louder than the depths of my education, experience, or my voice ever could.

One thing that grounds me is focusing on God's love and the saving grace of Jesus Christ. I remember and remind myself that Jesus fought this fight too. Every time I think of complaining, or rolling up my sleeves and symbolically clenching my fists, I ask myself, *What will it solve?*

I remind myself that Jesus came to earth not only for there to be abundant life, but to bridge the gaps that "difference" creates. Jesus left His throne, seated at the right hand of God, to redeem a lost world back to the Father. He didn't come for any particular ethnic group or color. He didn't come for only firstborn males or only-born females.

So why then are so many of us confused, thinking we are more saved and are of an elite group when we aren't as diverse as we ought to be? Because all we see at our Sunday services are people who look just like us? All we see is "the old neighborhood." Why do we so easily get things twisted, thinking our sorority/fraternity is the best in the nation when in fact God's grace and mercy is boundless, timeless, and holds no designated distinctions?

He came so everyone, all people, anyone who fits in the race called human who wants it, with no coercion, can have access to eternal life. Instead of projecting our biases or succumbing to the pain of the prejudices perpetrated against us, let's reflect on the fact that it wasn't because He was a Jew and had hair of wool, but because of His blood that we all have access, unadulterated access, to the glory and righteousness of God, and all that the friendship with Him entails. It is through and by His blood that those of us who are saved, baptized believers in Christ Jesus, are not only sons of God but are also "blood brothers/sisters," joint-heirs to the kingdom that is of the one true and living God. The message of colorlessness, or shall we say "blood-ness," is profound, yet simple, and has been illuminated in the lyrics of "The Blood Song" by Kirk Franklin. As believers we are all bound together by Christ's blood.

Sometimes we are faced with the unfortunate circumstance of life slapping us in the face. It doesn't matter how many times the experiences resemble something that happened before, we are thrown off guard and not prepared. We are then placed in the handicapping position of complaint. Because we may not know how to handle the issues

> Unfortunately, the depth of my skin color speaks louder than the depths of my education, experience, or my voice ever could.

I remind myself that Jesus came to earth not only for there to be abundant life, but to bridge the gaps that "difference" creates.

or address the problems, we often feel there is nothing to do but complain and blame. We are knocked off of our feet and left feeling like we can't go any further or we don't want to try anymore. We settle into disenfranchisement, disenchantment, and even marginalization and victimization. We may even find ourselves bordering on hopelessness, feeling as if things aren't going to change so why bother.

Regardless from which direction the blow comes, from work or school, home or church, ministry related or the world at large, we have to realize that it's not about us. It has never been about us. Rather it is and has always been about glorifying God in all we do.

Fortunately, we are not going to be able to please everybody. I'm blessed in knowing there is only the One who needs to get the glory and no one else. Colossians reminds us to do all things heartily, "as to the Lord and not to men, knowing that from the Lord you will receive the reward of the inheritance; for you serve the Lord Christ" (3:23–24 NKJV).

Wisdom Truth

For He himself is our peace, who has made us both one and has broken down in His flesh the dividing wall of hostility. (Ephesians 2:14 ESV)

For you are all sons of God through faith in Christ Jesus. For as many of you as were baptized into Christ have put on Christ. There is neither Jew nor Greek, there is neither slave nor free, there is neither male nor female; for you are all one in Christ Jesus. (Galatians 3:26–28 NKJV)

Wisdom Prayer

Father, Abba Father, Daddy, we need You like never before. The world is hungry for satisfaction but devoid of true understanding of who You are and our need for You. Father draw us nearer and give us the wherewithal to seek You instead of selfish superiority, worldly pleasures, greed, and hatred. Father, show us the need for togetherness, community, compassion, and communion with You. Thank You for Jesus Christ, Your Son and my Brother, and His sacrifice that gives us access to Your kingdom.

Regardless from which direction the blow comes, from work or school, home or church, ministry related or the world at large, we have to realize that it's not about us. It has never been about us. Rather it is and has always been about glorifying God in all that we do.

- What do you do when it seems discrimination wants to get the best of you?
- What godly truths do you recite to affirm you and the place you're in?
- When you consider the circumstance that has knocked you down, rather than staying down, get up, dust off, and keep moving. No need to complain or be handicapped.
- God knows what is best for you. He will join you in your storms as He is your umbrella. He has you covered.

_____

_____

_____

_____

_____

_____

_____

_____

_____

_____

_____

_____

Jamila Jenkins is a wife, mother, certified life coach, and entrepreneur. Alongside her husband, she co-pastors a church in Georgia. She teaches on resilience, admonishing others to "Do what you can, then stretch!" She is currently mapping out the details for her blog and podcast. Connect with Jamila on Facebook, Instagram, or via myencounterlife.com.

Chapter Twenty-Two

Let It Shine
Stacee P. Carr

I can still remember singing "This Little Light of Mine" in Sunday school as a child and during the weekly children's hour. The song was easy to learn because of its repetitive lyrics, and we sang them loud and proud. But although the song was in weekly rotation at our church, sadly we did not fully understand the significance of its words. For this song wasn't just a staple gospel chorus, but it served as the anthem of the historic civil rights movement when activists protested against the injustice of African Americans. This was the song they belted out in the face of police brutality, vicious dogs, water hoses, various items launched at their heads, vulgar threats, and harsh looks.

Containing an underlying message that protesters would be the guiding light to show America the vision of a better world, this song empowered African Americans to keep marching toward their freedom: freedom from racial segregation, disenfranchisement, and institutionalized racial discrimination.

This wasn't the first time African Americans sang a song for more than just expression, but its origin can be traced back hundreds of years. In the 1800s, certain songs were sung to assist fugitive slaves who traveled by way of the Underground Railroad. In order to outsmart those who desired to keep them bound in chains, songs secretly navigated the flight to freedom in the harsh cold of night. Songs like "Follow the Drinking Gourd" instructed runaway slaves to use the Big Dipper as a point of reference in making their way north.

Other songs led to secret station masters who owned or kept safe houses that were used by slaves as hideaways. Lit lanterns that hung outside the doors distinguished safe houses from all others. These lights gave slaves hope in the midst of the darkest night. Serving as a clearinghouse of information, station masters provided direction for all those who sought safety under their roofs, while lovingly guiding them to freedom.

Just as those station masters were positioned to light the way to freedom, we as Christians escort all who are bound in any sense to freedom in Jesus Christ. We are the safe houses identified by the light that we carry. As the light, we have a responsibility to shine. That's what lights do—shine. To accurately operate as the light, we must know the functions, the duties, and the role of the light.

In Matthew 5, Jesus gives us a clear depiction of the great power we possess as His light agents in the world.

Our first and foremost assignment is to illuminate. We do this by enlightening others about God's precepts. We, His disciples, are appointed to release godly knowledge that works to increase understanding of God and His will. With the world immersed in ignorance, sin, and misery, we aid in its reformation by the words we teach and by the lives we live.

People perish due to a lack of knowledge, but when they are exposed to the light, they are saved from destruction. This is not just physical and mental destruction, but also from the eternal destruction of soul and spirit. Acting as a guide, the light allows others to see the right path to take.

> Just as those station masters were positioned to light the way to freedom, we as Christians escort all who are bound in any sense to freedom in Jesus Christ.

God's Word is a light that shines on the road we tread so we may correctly see the path and any danger ahead. It even prevents our stumbling over obstacles, or falling down trenches, as it uncovers things hidden under the power of darkness. For light has the power to destroy all manner of darkness—depression, fear, anxiety, betrayal, discrimination, racism, or injustice.

We, the illuminators, are likened to a city that is set on a hill. In other words, we are obvious to every eye. Even people who don't want to, or who try not to see us, have no other choice but to view us because of our position. We just can't help ourselves. God has set us, settled us, and built us on an elevated place. We are not on the unbeliever's level. God has strategically exalted us so we can provide help to those in need. He tells us we are seated with Him in "heavenly places."

For this reason, our minds don't reside in the gutter, and low self-esteem has no right in us, due to the location where we are seated. It's not that we are better than others, just preferred. Being preferred is "to be picked out, favored, and to stand out among others." We stand out because God wants us to be seen, so He can get the glory out of our lives. That's why He positioned us upward, to be looked upon and admired.

He wants us on display to bring out the God colors in the world. We do this by shining on all those we encounter and performing good deeds that bring attention to God. Through us He becomes visible, and people can see Him at work in the earth.

We are posted as if on a candlestick, able to give light to all who seek knowledge under our rays. When one puts a light underneath something, it is concealed and restricted from permeating outward. Its full potential to impact its surroundings is halted. In like manner, God has not conveyed His grace and truth to us merely for our own use, but also for others. All we have to do is shine or be who God already set us up to be, just by operating in our light assignment.

The source of our light dwells on the inside of every believer. It is Jesus, whose life is the light of all mankind. We believe in the Light, and thus live in His likeness,

If this world never needed us to shine before, surely it needs us now.

being made one in Him. As a result, we become children of His Father. For we have been delivered from darkness by being exposed to God's truth. Yes, we have been illuminated and are thus instructed to live in a way as to illuminate others.

Anything that is illuminated becomes a light. So when we speak the word of truth over others' lives, we impart into them what we possess, which is Jesus, and they become as we are, lights. That's why it's important to do as the anthem says and let our light shine on everyone.

It's the basic principle of reciprocity, light begets light. In this fashion, the Great Commission is fulfilled. We are the burning, shining lights of the world. If this world never needed us to shine before, surely it needs us now. We are needed to help modify misguided thoughts and behaviors in regard to equality and what really matters. We are needed to reveal the truth of all people being created in the image and likeness of God. Every color, every hue, every shade is connected, is important, and should be treated as such.

A light that can do so much is not so little after all. In fact, it's great! It's so great that instead of reciting this unifying affirmation as usual, I'm going to sing it like this: "This *great* light of mine, I'm gonna let it shine! Let it shine, let it shine, let it shine!"

Wisdom Truth

In the same way, let your light shine before others, that they may see your good deeds and glorify your Father in heaven. (Matthew 5:16 NIV)

Wisdom Prayer

Heavenly Father, I thank You for Your light that lives within me. Help me to always let it shine so You might be visible to the world.

He wants us on display to bring out the God colors in the world.

- What is our role as God's light agents in the world?
- How do we make God visible in the earth?
- Name a situation that is in need of your light right now.

_____

_____

_____

_____

_____

_____

_____

_____

_____

_____

_____

_____

_____

_____

Stacee P. Carr is a preacher, speaker, teacher, psalmist, and author of *I AM*. She is an educated servant of God with a master's of divinity degree from North Carolina Theological Seminary. Writing is one of several abilities God has gifted her with in order to enlighten, empower, and strengthen *all* people. Stacee is married to associate pastor Richard, and they have two children. Connect with Stacee at staceepcarr.com and on Facebook, Instagram, and Twitter at @staceepcarr.

Chapter Twenty-Three

The White Supremacist in Me

Christina Custodio

Not long ago, I read something that stopped me dead in my tracks. I feel shame over it, but I feel it's important to share because it might give you a different perspective.

Through all the conversations we've been having, I have never felt the need to ask any questions of the white community. Because of how and where I grew up, I felt I knew the answers. The white community has been "my community." I have always been an introspective person who is honest with herself, and I didn't think there was much I needed to learn about myself—until I read this: "White supremacy can also infiltrate the thinking of people of color and is seen walked out through internalized racism, colorism, and other such manifestations."[4]

This was like a punch in the gut. As tears came to my eyes, I immediately knew what this meant, and how it applied to me. How in the world could I grow up as a Black girl with a white supremacist attitude? Believe me when I say this might be one of the hardest things I have ever admitted in my life, but it is my disturbing reality.

Growing up in Southern California through the 1980s, I was immersed in a predominately white world. Pop culture through magazines, movies, television,

How in the world could I grow up as a Black girl with a white supremacist attitude?

newspapers, and dolls told me the gold standard of beauty in this country was long, silky, flowing hair, a narrow nose, skinny body, thin lips, and light eyes.

I wasn't any of that.

I had short kinky hair, a wide nose, thick legs, full lips, and close-to-black eyes. Because I didn't look like what pop culture told me was beautiful, I assumed I was ugly—but not ugly enough not to be pushed to date the only Black boy in my whole junior-high school, while my beautiful Barbie-doll-like friends had a plethora of choices.

There were a few exceptions, but the predominant portrayal of people who looked like me was less than positive. We were seen as violent criminals, rapists, welfare babies, thugs, aggressive, and lazy. If we weren't that, then we were comedians, dancers, athletes, singers, or any job meant to entertain. I wasn't any of those things, so I just tried to fit into a world of white perfection.

I had a skewed perception of myself through lenses that didn't belong to me.

I didn't know what self-hate was, but I knew I wished I looked like the other girls in my school and models on TV and in magazines. Maybe then I would feel worthy of the places I found myself in.

I wanted to be white. I just knew if I were, I would be worthy to have a boyfriend just like all my girlfriends did. Of course, not one of them knew of my discontent. I feigned satisfaction with the position of "note carrier" of love notes and deliverer of secret admirer gifts from the boys who liked my friends but never considered me.

There were times when I thought maybe a boy thought of me as more than a friend. I dreamed of it, but none were ever brave enough to admit they liked the Black girl. I even prayed God would lighten my skin to make me tolerable. I spent many evenings with a bath towel draped over my head, secured by bobby pins on either side, pretending I had long flowing hair, while I flirted with my imaginary boyfriend in the mirror.

More self-hate.

I was not aware of the subtle spiral downward to the pit where I began to hate what I believed my skin represented.

But what does the Creator say?

> Then God said, "Let us make mankind in our image, in our like-
> ness, so that they may rule over the fish in the sea and the birds in
> the sky, over the livestock and all the wild animals, and over all the
> creatures that move along the ground." So God created mankind
> in his own image, in the image of God he created them; male and
> female he created them. (Genesis 1:26–27 NIV)

As a young impressionable girl, that wasn't enough to pull me out of the pit of self-hatred. I'm not sure I felt included in that Scripture. Black people didn't reign over anything. Maybe I wasn't a part of this story after all.

During my sophomore year of high school, my school had a talent show where kids were allowed to dress up. A boy who dated one of my best friends came dressed as Michael Jackson (the Black version). I knew him to be a nice kid. He showed up in full "blackface" with a black wig, brown face, neck, arms, and fingers. He sprinted over to me, put his arm around me, and said, "Hey, Christina! We can totally date now!"

What did that mean? Is that something he had secretly desired? Was he making fun of me? I didn't know how to feel, so I just laughed, and through my smile felt self-hate.

Even now, I fight back tears and shame.

Fast forward to the summer after I graduated from high school in Ohio. My very wise mother signed me up to attend a minority summer program called LINKS at Ohio University, where I would be attending that fall. I was horrified! I pleaded with her not to make me go. I didn't have anything in common with those Black kids. I would be uncomfortable. None of them grew up like me. I wasn't going to fit in. I thought I was better than they were.

"Don't make me gooooooo!"

My mom knew what I needed, and my reaction probably solidi-fied her decision. When I got there, I was scared to death. However, my I wanted to be white. I just knew if I were, I would be worthy to have a boyfriend just like all my girlfriends did.

Black-girl-raised-in-a-white-world sonar must have gone off. Very quickly, I met a few girls who were raised just like me. I was surprised to find we all had one thing in common, although we came from many different backgrounds, places, and situations. We knew the struggle of what it was like to live in this country with skin like ours. For the first time in my life, I felt like I belonged. I didn't have to explain, I didn't have to suppress, I didn't have to pretend. For one whole week, I could just be me.

When I started school in the fall, I was excited to be back with my new "brothers and sisters." During my first semester of school, I even took some classes to learn more about the people I was growing to love more and more each day. Black history, Black media, and even Swahili classes all introduced me to a story I had never been told in school. After my first Black history class, I came out angry. I never knew we were kings and queens in Africa. I never knew we invented so many of the things in the world we all use every day. We did more than find three hundred uses for the peanut!

I had a hard time looking at the majority around me who I felt had robbed me of knowing the glorious past of my people. We were more than slaves. We were more, but I still had seventeen years of a different version of us ingrained into my mind. At least I had a new image to combat it with.

Although I saw some improvements over the next twenty-nine years, those negative images of who my people were and continue to be, came face to face with a different narrative of who magazines, TV, internet, movies, etc. have portrayed us to be. Those (like me before college) who have lived much of their life in a community with very little interaction with people of color from all backgrounds and experiences can only count on what they are shown and told to believe.

> For the first time in my life, I felt like I belonged. I didn't have to explain, I didn't have to suppress, I didn't have to pretend. For one whole week, I could just be me.

It pains me to confess I *still* must fight against believing stereotypes of my own people due to the images that to this day remain in my head. However, I have learned that my first thought is what society has conditioned me to think; my second thought defines who I am.

I thank God that today I know the truth. I choose to take every one of my thoughts captive and make them obedient to Christ (2 Corinthians 10:5) who tells me that we are "fearfully and wonderfully made" (Psalm 139:14 NIV).

I am a proud Black woman. I love my brown skin. I love who I am and who we are as a people and continue to be.

We are all made in His image—red, yellow, black, and white. And God does not make mistakes.

I pray for so many who still struggle to see all of God's people, including themselves, as His beautiful creations.

Now I ask, if that happened to me, what do you think it did to you?

> I choose to take every one of my thoughts captive and make them obedient to Christ.

Wisdom Truth

Therefore if you have any encouragement from being united with Christ, if any comfort from his love, if any common sharing in the Spirit, if any tenderness and compassion, then make my joy complete by being like-minded, having the same love, being one in spirit and of one mind. Do nothing out of selfish ambition or vain conceit. Rather, in humility value others above yourselves, not looking to your own interests but each of you to the interests of the others. (Philippians 2:1–4 NIV)

Wisdom Prayer

Dear Heavenly Father, Today I offer up my heart to You. I confess that I have held sinful thoughts about myself and others. Lord, give me eyes to see what You see, allow me to hear what You hear, and allow me to love who You love. I know I am fearfully and wonderfully made and there is no one else like me. Thank You for creating me to be a unique and loved child of Yours. Thank You for making each of us an important part of the body. Help us use the gifts we've been given to encourage each other and grow Your kingdom in love. You are a good, good Father, and I offer my life to You.

⌁ Wisdom Reflection

- Is there anything negative in your life you have believed that goes against what God says in His Word?
- Has there been a place God has called you where you didn't to go, but you found it was just what you needed?
- How did it change you? Is there something about yourself you need to learn to love?

_____

_____

_____

_____

_____

_____

_____

_____

Christina Custodio is a wife and mother of three. She is the founder of Agapeland Ministries, dedicated to inspiring women to find joy regardless of their circumstances. Christina is the author of *Too Much Cream in My Coffee*, a book to help foster racial reconciliation, and she is currently working on a book recounting the forty-four days she lived in a hospital following her son's near death. Visit Christina at christinacustodio.com.

Resources

Be the Bridge: Pursuing God's Heart for Racial Reconciliation
Latasha Morrison
Waterbrook (2019)
Website: www.bethebridge.com

The Colors of Culture: The Beauty of Diverse Friendships
Melindajoy Mingo
IVP (2020)

The Third Option: Hope for a Racially Divided Nation
Miles McPherson
Howard Books (2020)

White Awake: An Honest Look at What it Means to Be White
Daniel Hill
IVP Books (2017)

The Book of Forgiving: The Fourfold Path of Healing Ourselves and Our World
Desmond Tutu and Mpho Tutu
Harper One (2015)

I'm Still Here: Black Dignity in a World Made for Whiteness
Austin Channing Brown
Convergent Books (2018)

Divided by Faith: Evangelical Religion and the Problem of Race in America
Michael O. Emerson
Oxford University Press (2001)

Oneness Embraced: Reconciliation, the Kingdom, and How We are Stronger Together
Tony Evans
Moody Publishers (2015)

One Blood: Parting Words to the Church on Race and Love
John M. Perkins
Moody Publishers (2018)

So You Want to Talk about Race
Ijeoma Oluo
Seal Press (2018)

Endnotes

1. George Linnaeus Banks, "What I Live For," *The World's Best Poetry*, vol. 4, *The Higher Life*, Bliss Carman, ed. (Philadelphia: John D. Morris and Co.).
2. Matthew Henry, *Matthew Henry's Concise Commentary on the Whole Bible* (Nashville: Thomas Nelson), 2003.
3. Mary Fairchild, "What God's Grace Means to Christians," *Learn Religions*, www.learnreligions.com/meaning-of-gods-grace-for-christians-700723.
4. Be the Bridge, https://bethebridge.com/get-started/.

She Writes for Him

ROMANS 8:28
BOOKS
AN IMPRINT OF REDEMPTION PRESS

To order additional copies of this book, please visit

www.redemption-press.com.
Also available on Amazon.com
or by calling toll-free 1-844-2REDEEM.

Other books in this series:
She Writes for Him: Stories of Resilient Faith
She Writes for Him: Stories of Living Hope

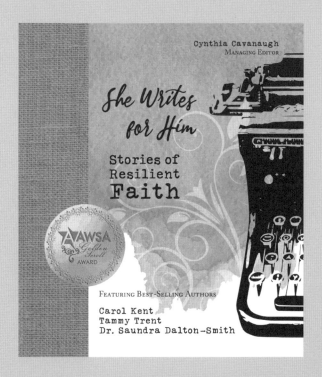

She Writes for Him: Stories of Resilient Faith is the debut book in the She Writes for Him Series and winner of the 2020 AWSA Golden Scroll Award.

Written by thirty brave women who have boldly ventured out to tell their hard stories believing God can be trusted in the midst of tragic circumstances. They found God's redemption through their pain and stories of abortion, shame, betrayal, depression, anxiety, and loss.